MOHANDAS GANDHI

MODERN SPIRITUAL MASTERS
Robert Ellsberg, Series Editor

This series introduces the writing and vision of some of the great spiritual masters of the twentieth century. Along with selections from their writings, each volume includes a comprehensive introduction, presenting the author's life and writings in context and drawing attention to points of special relevance to contemporary spirituality.

Some of these authors found a wide audience in their lifetimes. In other cases recognition has come long after their deaths. Some are rooted in long-established traditions of spirituality. Others charted new, untested paths. In each case, however, the authors in this series have engaged in a spiritual journey shaped by the influences and concerns of our age. Such concerns include the challenges of modern science, religious pluralism, secularism, and the quest for social justice.

At the dawn of a new millennium this series commends these modern spiritual masters, along with the saints and witnesses of previous centuries, as guides and companions to a new generation of seekers.

Already published:
Dietrich Bonhoeffer (edited by Robert Coles)
Simone Weil (edited by Eric O. Springsted)
Henri Nouwen (edited by Robert A. Jonas)
Pierre Teilhard de Chardin (edited by Ursula King)
Anthony de Mello (edited by William Dych, S.J.)
Charles de Foucauld (edited by Robert Ellsberg)
Oscar Romero (by Marie Dennis, Rennie Golden,
      and Scott Wright)
Eberhard Arnold (edited by Johann Christoph Arnold)
Thomas Merton (edited by Christine M. Bochen)
Thich Nhat Hanh (edited by Robert Ellsberg)
Rufus Jones (edited by Kerry Walters)
Mother Teresa (edited by Jean Maalouf)
Edith Stein (edited by John Sullivan, O.C.D.)
John Main (edited by Laurence Freeman)

Forthcoming volumes include:
Flannery O'Connor
G. K. Chesterton

MODERN SPIRITUAL MASTERS SERIES

MOHANDAS GANDHI

Essential Writings

Selected
with an Introduction by
JOHN DEAR

ORBIS BOOKS

Maryknoll, New York 10545

Second printing March 2003

Library of Congress Cataloging-in-Publication Data
Gandhi, Mahatma, 1869-1948.
    [Selections. 2002]
    Mohandas Gandhi : essential writings / selected with an introduction
by John Dear.
       p.   cm. – (Modern spiritual masters series)
    Includes bibliographical references.
    ISBN 1-57075-432-2 (pbk.)
    I. Dear, John, 1959- II. Title. III. Series.
DS481.G3 A25 2002
954.03′5′092 – dc21

                                       2002003388

For
Kathy Kelly,
Simon Harak, S.J.,
Danny Muller,
and "Voices in the Wilderness,"
with gratitude and hope for peace
with the people of Iraq

Contents

Chronology of the Life of Mohandas Gandhi

1869   October 2. Mohandas Karamchand Gandhi born to Karamchand and Putlibai Gandhi in Porbandar, India.

1882   At age thirteen, marries Kasturbai Makanji.

1888   September 4. Sails to London to study law.

1891   June 11. Admitted to the bar, becomes a lawyer, and sails back to India the next day.

1893   April. Moves to Durban, South Africa, to practice law. One week after his arrival, he is thrown off a train for refusing to move to the third-class section because of his skin color and decides to spend all his energy fighting racism and injustice.

1904   Founds weekly newspaper, *Indian Opinion*.

        Buys one hundred acres near Durban and founds Phoenix Farm, his first ashram.

1906   September 11. Gives a stirring speech at a mass meeting in Johannesburg, inspiring thousands of Indians to disobey racist laws.

        Professes a vow of celibacy.

        Publishes *Hind Swaraj* ("Indian Home Rule") calling for India's independence and return to village life.

1908   January 10. Undergoes first arrest and first night in jail, in Johannesburg; adopts the term satyagraha and encourages Indians to burn registration cards.

1909   Begins correspondence with Tolstoy.

1910   Buys eleven hundred acres near Johannesburg and establishes Tolstoy Farm, his second ashram.

1913   Leads the great march from Newcastle to Volksrust and is arrested.

1914   Negotiates the Indian Relief Act with the South African government.

        July 18. Leaves South Africa and visits England.

1915   January 9. Returns to India.

1916   Establishes Satyagraha Ashram near Ahmedabad; travels throughout India.

1917   Begins campaign in Champaran on behalf of poor sharecroppers; attracts national attention.

1918   Leads the textile workers strike in Ahmedabad.

1919   April 6. Calls for a national strike, a day of prayer and fasting; India shuts down.

        April 13. British soldiers massacre 379 peaceful protesters in Amritsar.

        Founds two newspapers, *Navajivan* and *Young India*.

1920   Reorganizes the Indian Congress Party, launches the Satyagraha Campaign, and the independence movement begins anew.

1922   Suspends civil disobedience campaign due to violence, but is arrested.

        March 18. At the Great Trial, sentenced to six years.

1924   February 5. Released from prison because of poor health.

        Conducts twenty-one-day fast for Hindu-Muslim unity.

1926   Begins his autobiography, *The Story of My Experiments with Truth.*

1930   March 12–April 6. Carries out Salt March to Dandi; launches new Satyagraha campaign.

       May 4. Arrested and imprisoned.

1931   August–December. Attends Round Table conference in London.

1932   January 4. Arrested and imprisoned one week after returning from England.

       September 20. Declares a fast to the death to end "untouchability."

1933   May. Released from prison after beginning another twenty-one-day fast.

       Leaves Sabarmati Ashram and moves to Wardha; begins nationwide tour; founds a journal, *Harijan.*

1935   Builds "Sevagram," or model village, in Wardha.

1942   August 8. Calls for new civil disobedience against British rule.

       August 9. Arrested and imprisoned.

1944   February 22. Kasturbai dies in prison with Gandhi at her side.

       May 6. Released from prison.

1946   August. Begins six-month peacemaking walk through war-torn Noakhali.

1947   August 15. India wins independence; Gandhi prays and fasts for unity and nonviolence.

       September 1. Undertakes a "fast unto death" to stop brutal riots and massacres in Calcutta; three days later, when the violence ends, Gandhi breaks the fast.

1948   January 13. Begins a fast to the death to stop the
        violence in Delhi.

        January 30. At age seventy-nine, Mohandas Gandhi is
        assassinated in Delhi as he walks to evening prayer.

Sources and Recommended Readings

The Collected Works of Mahatma Gandhi. 95 vols. Ahmedabad: Navajivan Pub., 1967–84. (All citations in this book are taken from the *Collected Works,* with the volume number and the date of the passage noted, unless otherwise indicated.)

The Selected Works of Mahatma Gandhi. 6 vols. Edited by Shriman Navayan. Ahmedabad: Navajivan Pub., 1968.

Selections from Gandhi. Ahmedabad: Navajivan Pub., 1957.

Gandhi, M. K. *All Men Are Brothers.* New York: Continuum, 1980.

———. *My Religion.* Ahmedabad: Navajivan Pub., 1968.

———. *Nonviolence in Peace and War.* 2 vols. Ahmedabad: Navajivan Pub., 1945, 1949.

———. *The Story of My Experiments in Truth: An Autobiography.* Boston: Beacon Press, 1957.

Mahatma Gandhi: Letters to Americans. Edited by Dr. E. S. Reddy. New York: Bharatiya Vidya Bhavan, 1998.

Recommended Biographies

Brown, Judith M. *Gandhi: Prisoner of Hope.* New Haven: Yale University Press, 1989.

Chadha, Yogesh. *Gandhi: A Life.* New York: John Wiley, 1997.

Easwaran, Eknath. *Gandhi the Man.* Petaluma, Calif.: Nilgiri Press, 1997.

Fischer, Louis. *The Life of Mahatma Gandhi.* New York: Harper & Row, 1950.

Holmes, John Haynes. *My Gandhi.* New York: Harper & Brothers, 1953.

Payne, Robert. *The Life and Death of Mahatma Gandhi.* New York: E. P. Dutton, 1969.

Sheean, Vincent. *Lead, Kindly Light.* New York: Random House, 1949.

Wolpert, Stanley. *Gandhi's Passion.* New York: Oxford University Press, 2001.

Introduction

Mahatma Gandhi, Apostle of Nonviolence

When Mahatma Gandhi was assassinated on January 30, 1948, the world hailed him as one of the greatest spiritual leaders, not just of the century, but of all time. He was ranked with Thoreau, Tolstoy, and St. Francis, but also with Buddha, Mohammed, and even Jesus. "Generations to come will scarce believe that such a one as this ever in flesh and blood walked upon this earth," Albert Einstein wrote at the time.

Gandhi's legacy includes the brilliantly waged struggle against institutionalized racism in South Africa, the independence movement of India, and a groundbreaking path of interreligious dialogue, but it also boasts the first widespread application of nonviolence as *the* most powerful tool for positive social change. Gandhi's nonviolence was not simply political: it was rooted and grounded in the spiritual, which is why he exploded beyond India's political stage and onto the world stage, for his own lifetime and for all times.

Gandhi was, first and foremost, a religious man in search of God. For more than fifty years, he pursued truth, proclaiming that the best way to discover truth is through the practice of active, faith-based nonviolence.

I discovered Gandhi when I was a Jesuit novice at the Jesuit novitiate in Wernersville, Pennsylvania. My friends and I were passionately interested in peace and justice issues, so we undertook a detailed study of Gandhi. We were amazed to learn that Gandhi professed fourteen vows, even as we were preparing to profess vows of poverty, chastity, and obedience. I added a fourth vow — under Gandhi's influence — a vow of nonviolence, which Gandhi had professed in 1907. My friends and I undertook our own Gandhian experiments in truth and nonviolence, with prayer, discussions, fasting, and public witness, followed by serious reflection. We looked to Gandhi for ways to change our own culture of violence.

Gandhi has helped me enormously over the years in my work for peace, interreligious dialogue, civil disobedience, and opposition to nuclear weapons. When I was imprisoned for an anti-nuclear demonstration for eight months, I studied Gandhi again to see how he survived prison and understood civil disobedience. For more than two decades, I have read Gandhi's writings and biographies to find clues about how to live humanly in our inhuman world. Gandhi's answer is always the same: steadfast, persistent, dedicated, committed, patient, relentless, truthful, prayerful, loving, active nonviolence.

For example, a twenty-one-year-old British student activist named Ronald Duncan wrote a pamphlet about a labor strike he organized and mailed copies to over one hundred activists around the world. Only Gandhi replied, explaining that the means are the ends, and that all our organizing must be nonviolent to the core.

Duncan responded by asking Gandhi if he could someday come to India for a visit. Gandhi immediately sent a cable saying, "Meet me at Wardha on the 23rd." With the fundraising support of friends, Duncan set off to India, arrived in the village of Wardha, and hired a taxi to the ashram. On the journey through the barren countryside, Gandhi appeared alone on the road. He had walked three miles by himself to meet the young student. Gandhi was in his late sixties at the time.

"As I was saying in my letter," Gandhi said without missing a beat, "means must determine ends, and indeed it's questionable whether there is an end. The best we can do is to make sure of the method and examine our motives."

They walked back, discussing nonviolence. There were no introductions or questions about the trip. Gandhi picked up as if they were old friends, engaged in passionate discussion. That's Gandhi: single-minded devotion to nonviolence. Duncan was profoundly impressed.

According to all the accounts I have read, Gandhi had that effect on everyone. He kept trying to plumb the depths of nonviolence, beginning with his own heart and soul. Along the way, he unleashed a new method of social change, which he called satyagraha (from the Sanskrit for "truth force"). He led a movement against racial injustice in South Africa and then brought about a nonviolent revolution in India that secured independence from the British empire. His example and teachings inspire us to apply the same single-mindedness in our pursuit of an end to war, nuclear weapons, environmental destruction, violence, hunger, poverty, and injustice, and the creation of a culture of peace, justice, and nonviolence. In other words, he challenges us to become prophets and apostles of nonviolence.

Gandhi's Life in South Africa

Gandhi experimented with his life as few others have. He strived to renounce every trace of selfishness and violence within himself in a relentless pursuit of truth. While he was plumbing his own depths of nonviolence, he realized that he also had to pursue the practice of nonviolence as widely as possible in the public sphere in the pursuit of peace and justice for the poor. He was at once a devoutly spiritual, religious person as well as an astute politician. He introduced an entirely new way to organize and run nations and to transform cultures of violence into cultures of nonviolence.

Gandhi's transformation was a slow, painful process of daily renunciation, prayer, study, and radical experimentation with his own life at great personal cost. He was born in a small seaside town in India on October 2, 1869, to a proud businessman and a devout mother who fasted regularly and prayed constantly. A shy boy, he was married at age thirteen to a girl named Kasturbai, in a marriage arranged by their parents. At age eighteen, he was shipped off to law school in England, where at first he tried to become the perfect Westerner, even learning how to dance and play the violin. When he returned to India in 1891, he was unable to find a job, so his relatives suggested he pursue an offer to practice law for the Indian community in South Africa. Desperate and excited, he boarded a ship to South Africa in 1893.

Fifty years later, a Christian minister asked Gandhi what the most transformative experience was in his life. Gandhi told the story of his first week in South Africa. He was traveling overnight by train to conduct a case in Pretoria. He was quietly reading in a first-class compartment when a white conductor appeared at the door and ordered him to move immediately to a third-class compartment or be thrown off the train. Gandhi found himself face to face with institutionalized racism. He refused to budge, so they beat him up and threw him off the train. He sat all night in the freezing cold on the train platform in the middle of nowhere weighing his options. He could return to India, or he could join the handful of violent revolutionaries who seek change through bloodshed, or he could pursue a third path: peaceful, prayerful, public confrontation with legalized racism until everyone's civil rights were honored.

"The train steamed away leaving me shivering in the cold," Gandhi recalled. "The creative experience comes there. I was afraid for my very life. I entered the dark waiting room. There was a white man in the room. I was afraid of him. What was my duty, I asked myself. Should I go back to India, or should I go forward, with God as my helper, and face whatever was in store for me? I decided to stay and suffer. My active nonviolence began from that date. And God put me through the test during that very journey. That was one of the richest experiences of my life."

The next day, Gandhi began organizing key leaders within the Indian community to speak out publicly against segregation. When he turned twenty-five, he won the law case that had originally brought him to South Africa and planned to return home to India. But the day of his departure, the South African government announced that Indians would no longer be allowed to vote. At the huge farewell party organized in his honor that night, Gandhi's friends pleaded with him to stay and help them fight for their civil rights. He stayed in South Africa for twenty more years.

Indians in South Africa had been denied basic civil rights, including the right to vote. Gandhi organized widespread non-violent resistance to these injustices. He defended hundreds of clients, wrote countless articles and press statements against these unjust laws, and spoke to any group that would listen. Then in 1906, the Transvaal South African government announced it was considering new legislation that would require every Indian to register with the government, be fingerprinted, and carry a cer-tificate of registration at all times. The Indian community was stunned.

On September 11, 1906, Gandhi called a mass meeting in Jo-hannesburg to protest the proposed legislation. Three thousand people filled the Empire Theater. Gandhi was not sure what he would say, until one of the preliminary speakers made an offhand remark, announcing that he would resist these unjust laws "in the name of God" even if it meant his death. That was the answer. Gandhi stood up and declared that if everyone present took a vow of nonviolent resistance to these unjust laws, and remained faithful to their pledge and to God, even if they were arrested, imprisoned, tortured, and killed, the struggle would be won. It was as simple as that. Their voluntary suffering would attract the sympathy of the world and melt the hearts of white South Africans. The audience was captivated. They rose as one and took a vow of nonviolent resistance to the proposed legislation. Within a matter of months, over fifteen hundred Indians were ar-rested and imprisoned for opposing the "pass laws." Thus was born the Satyagraha movement. (Excerpts from Gandhi's famous speech are included below, pp. 150–52).

A short time later, in response to a letter Gandhi had written to him, Leo Tolstoy wrote to Gandhi that Gandhi was offering not just South Africa, but the whole world, a new way to fight injus-tice through the practice of loving resistance on a massive scale. Tolstoy had theorized and theologized about such a program, but Gandhi was living it. Gandhi wanted to find a word to describe this new method of opposing injustice, and so he organized a contest. Eventually, he coined the word himself, satyagraha, or "truth force." "Satyagraha means resisting untruth by truthful means," Gandhi explained in a speech in 1911. "It can be offered at any place, at any time, and by any person, even though he may be in a minority of one. If one remains steadfast in it, in a spirit of dedication, it always brings success. Satyagraha knows neither frustration nor despair."

When the Asiatic Registration Act became law in July 1907, Gandhi officially launched the Satyagraha Campaign. On January 10, 1908, Gandhi was arrested for the first time, and the next day he was sentenced to two months of hard labor in prison. It was his first prison term. On August 16, 1908, Gandhi publicly called for the burning of registration certificates. Indians throughout South Africa were inspired by Gandhi and joined his campaign. "They will put us in prison, they will torture us, and they will kill us," Gandhi told the Indian community, "but we will not fight back nor will we give in, and so, our victory is assured." Thousands marched and went to jail, and the oppressive white government was forced to back down. When Gandhi was arrested and imprisoned later that year, he studied Thoreau and drew the astonishing conclusion that "the real road to happiness lies in going to jail and undergoing sufferings and privations there in the interest of one's country and religion."

In 1913, the South African government announced that only Christian marriages were valid, in a blatant attack on the Indian community, which was largely Hindu and Muslim. Gandhi organized new marches and demonstrations, and Indians burned registration cards. As government repression intensified, Gandhi called upon Indians to accept whatever suffering they were forced to endure without flinching or retaliating. He held that the authorities, as well as the whole world, would eventually be forced to recognize the Indians' human dignity and the truth of their cause and give them justice. As the jails filled up and the world denounced the racist repression, the government caved in to the growing pressure.

On November 6, 1913, Gandhi led five thousand Indians,

primarily mine workers, in an illegal march from Natal to Transvaal. He was arrested and imprisoned on November 11 and sentenced to three months at hard labor. Like Nelson Mandela fifty years later, Gandhi spent those long prison days breaking rocks. But within months, the South African government gave in to the campaign, passed new legislation protecting the rights of all Indians, and set all the remaining political prisoners free. As the pass laws and other segregation laws were lifted and the prisoners released, the Indian community declared victory, not just for themselves, but for all South Africans.

•

Throughout their years in South Africa, Mohandas and Kasturbai raised four sons. One day, near the turn of the century, Gandhi visited a Trappist monastery outside of Johannesburg. He was so inspired by the life of intentional community, prayer, simplicity, and farming, that he considered forming his own religious community and farm. His reading of Ruskin's classic work *Unto This Last* pushed him to do it. In 1904 Gandhi purchased one hundred acres near Durban and created the Phoenix Settlement, his first ashram.

In 1910, as the movement exploded and hundreds sought to join his farm, he bought eleven hundred acres near Johannesburg and founded Tolstoy Farm, his second ashram, which became the center of the Satyagraha campaign and the support network for all political prisoners. Ashram community members grew their own food, built their own buildings, ran their own schools, pooled all their money, made their own clothes, prayed together, and shared everything in common. In an effort to be poor and simple, Gandhi walked nearly everywhere he went. For years, he walked nearly every day to Johannesburg — a twenty-one-mile hike, one way. Gandhi also started a national weekly newspaper to mobilize and organize the Indian community in their struggle for justice.

Just as he arrived on South Africa's political stage, Gandhi underwent a profound inner spiritual explosion. He studied Tolstoy, Thoreau, Emerson, the New Testament, and the Bhagavad Gita.

His reading of the religious scriptures, particularly of the Sermon on the Mount, deepened his convictions and gave him a moral and spiritual framework that determined the rest of his life. He committed his life to "seeking God face to face." In 1906, he professed lifelong vows of truth, nonviolence, celibacy, poverty, and fearlessness.

Gandhi's Struggle for India's Independence

On July 18, 1914, after negotiating a breakthrough settlement with the government, Gandhi left South Africa for good. He embarked on a trip to England and finally returned to India permanently on January 9, 1915, to a hero's welcome. Under the guidance of G. K. Gokhale, a revered politician, Gandhi spent his first year back rediscovering his homeland by crisscrossing the country, learning its problems and listening to the poor. He reacquainted himself with India's needs and potential and studied how he could apply the lessons of satyagraha learned in South Africa to India's struggle for independence from Britain.

Gandhi set up another ashram, on the Sabarmati river near Ahmedabad, where he lived for the next sixteen years. Over 250 people eventually joined his community, which practiced the same austerity he originally witnessed at the Trappist monastery in South Africa. Each member professed fourteen vows, including truth, nonviolence, celibacy, poverty, fearlessness, physical labor, tolerance of all religions, and making their own clothes. They prayed together, ate together, farmed the land, published newspapers, and prepared themselves to suffer and die in the nonviolent struggle for independence.

In 1917, a determined peasant from the other side of the country begged Gandhi to visit his desperately poor remote region (Champaran) and to help the starving peasants in their struggle against oppressive British landlords. Gandhi agreed, made the long journey by train, and quietly started gathering information about the specific injustices committed against the peasants. He expected to stay a month, but stayed nearly two years. One day, while he was riding along on an elephant, the British arrested him. Overnight, the news spread throughout the region that a holy man had been arrested while seeking their rights. Thousands of peasants gathered outside the courthouse to support Gandhi. He was immediately released, allowed to finish his study of illegal abuses against the farmworkers, and eventually the Indian government passed a new agrarian reform law to protect disenfranchised farmworkers. Gandhi became the hope of the Indian people.

On March 18, 1919, Britain announced that the repressive measures it set up during World War I against the Indian independence movement, restricting basic civil rights, would continue, even though the war was over. The Rowlatt Acts suppressed freedom of speech, press, and assembly, in an effort to crush the ever growing dissent. Gandhi announced the next day that he had a dream in which the whole nation had gone on strike against British rule, and he invited the whole nation to consider making his dream a reality. On April 6, in response to Gandhi's call for a general *hartal,* a national day of prayer and fasting, virtually everyone stayed at home to pray and fast, and India was shut down for a day. Millions marched in the streets to the stunned shock and amazement of the British (and Gandhi). Suddenly, India was waking up. The British government responded by doing what empires do — repressing the movement, arresting its leaders, killing demonstrators. The following week, British soldiers massacred 379 peaceful protesters and wounded another 1,200 in the city of Amritsar.

In the months that followed, Gandhi prayerfully decided to make a complete break with the British empire and dedicated the rest of his life to achieving India's independence through peaceful nonviolence. He called for massive "nonviolent noncooperation with the British, until they peacefully realize they are masters in someone else's house and leave." In 1920, Gandhi persuaded the Indian National Congress to adopt the strategy of satyagraha to achieve freedom, and the movement officially began. From 1920 to 1921, Gandhi called for widespread civil disobedience against British rule, but after a handful of demonstrators brutally killed twenty-one police officers in Chauri Chaura, Gandhi suspended the movement, infuriating other protest leaders. For the rest of his life, Gandhi would wrestle with the movement, calling off every campaign at the slightest outbreak of violence. In the end, he regretted that the Indian people were never as committed to nonviolence as he wanted them to be.

By 1922, over fifty thousand Indians were in prison for civil disobedience. When Gandhi called off the campaign, the British released all political prisoners, but then arrested Gandhi. On March 18, 1922, he was brought before a judge on the charge of sedition and invited to make a statement before he was sentenced. "Noncooperation with evil was as much a duty as cooperation with good," Gandhi said, and since British rule over India was evil, he declared, he was guilty of nonviolent noncooperation with it. Then he challenged the judge to give him the highest penalty possible or to resign and join the movement. Gandhi was sentenced to six years in prison, the maximum sentence.

For the next two years behind bars, Gandhi meditated, read hundreds of books, wrote countless letters, and worked on his spinning wheel each day. He also began writing his autobiography. Although the British government attempted to silence Gandhi, his imprisonment only raised his stature in the hearts of all Indians, who now called him "Mahatma," meaning "Great Soul."

Gandhi urged all those who risked arrest to embrace suffering with love as the path to political and spiritual freedom. "We must widen the prison gates," he wrote, "and we must enter them as a bridegroom enters the bride's chamber. Freedom is to be wooed only inside prison walls and sometimes on the gallows, never in the council chambers, courts, or the schoolroom."

On February 5, 1924, Gandhi was released from prison because of poor health. In the following years, while continuing his support for independence, he focused much of his time on reforming Indian life to prepare India for the coming of independence. His top priority was Hindu-Muslim unity. At one point, he undertook a grueling twenty-one-day fast for interreligious reconciliation and reformation, which inspired millions of Indians to relinquish past prejudices and pursue reconciliation. He called for the abolition of Hinduism's lowest caste, the untouchables, the poorest of the poor, who were consigned from birth until death to clean toilets. He advocated daily use of the spinning wheel to make one's own clothing and a boycott against British clothing. He campaigned for the development of "constructive programs," which would improve village life for ordinary, impoverished Indians. He toured the country, preaching nonviolence, and inspiring millions of Indians to change their lives and their nation. Occasionally he met with the current British viceroy and would announce that the time had come for Britain to leave India. Hundreds of thousands of people would turn out to catch a glimpse of the Mahatma wherever he appeared. If the crowd was loud or unruly, he would sit in silence for hours until everyone became perfectly still. Then he would quietly depart.

On March 2, 1930, Gandhi wrote to the viceroy and announced that unless Britain lifted the unjust salt tax that deprived millions of salt, he would embark on a campaign of civil disobedience. On March 12, Gandhi set off on a 240-mile march to the sea town of Dandi. Thousands of people turned out to greet the marchers, surprising even Gandhi. Each day, the tension and excitement mounted. On April 6, after his morning meditation, Gandhi bent down and picked up the illegal salt. The country exulted in jubilation. Hundreds of thousands of people began to pick up, make, sell, and distribute salt, thus violating the British salt tax and declaring their independence. Gandhi's simple gesture worked. It woke up the sleeping giant, and the days of British rule were numbered.

Within a month, the British arrested and imprisoned sixty thousand protesters, including all the leaders of the movement. Gandhi himself was arrested on May 4 and imprisoned for eight months. On May 20, two thousand satyagrahis marched to the Dharsana salt mines and approached the entrance in small groups in order to enter and demand their right to salt. As each group of Gandhian protesters approached, the British soldiers savagely beat them over the head with steel rods, seriously wounding hundreds and killing several of them. The world was horrified by reports of this vicious assault by the so-called "civilized" British empire upon unarmed, peaceful demonstrators who did not lift a hand in self-defense. Thousands more joined the protest. The British were quickly losing control and becoming ever more repressive. Within the year, the British imprisoned more than a hundred thousand Indians for nonviolent protest. Millions of people around the world began to call for the British to leave India.

In March 1931, in response to mounting pressure, the British released all political prisoners, recognized the right to boycott foreign-made cloth, and lifted the ban on home-made salt. They then invited Gandhi to England for a "Round Table" conference to discuss possible independence for India. Gandhi went to London, where he stayed for four months with Muriel Lester at Kingsley Hall in the poor East End section. Though there was no immediate political outcome from his efforts, Gandhi was able to put the case for independence to millions of British citizens and Europeans. He won them over with his sincerity, charm, and truth. Though many of his co-workers concluded that the conference was a failure, Gandhi felt that one should not refuse to meet with one's enemies. One week after he returned to India, on January 4, 1932, the British outlawed the Congress Party and imprisoned all its leaders, including Gandhi.

Gandhi continued to speak out for the abolition of the Hindu untouchable caste. On September 20, he began a "fast unto death" in his prison cell "for the removal of untouchability." The country was shocked. His friends, particularly Jawaharlal Nehru, said that untouchability had existed for thousands of years and such a fast was suicidal. But Indians revered Gandhi and trusted his wisdom. Almost immediately, Hindu leaders around the country welcomed untouchables into their temples for the first time in thousands of years. In just days, Hinduism underwent breathtaking reforms as the faithful feared the death of their mahatma. After five days, Gandhi ended his fast. He would continue his advocacy for the untouchables for the rest of his life, and Hinduism would never be the same.

Gandhi was released from prison in May 1933. He and Kasturbai decided to move their home to the poorest region in India, the tiny, inaccessible village of Wardha, located directly in India's center. Then he embarked on a full-time nationwide tour and campaign to reform Indian village life. For the next six years, Gandhi traveled the country, spoke to millions of people, fought poverty and illiteracy, urged use of the spinning wheel, and raised enormous amounts of money to support the untouchables, whom he now called "Harijans," or "Children of God." At several rallies, over two hundred thousand people turned up to watch Gandhi strike a match and burn huge mounds of British clothing.

Over the years, he built what he called a "model village," or "Sevagram," meaning "Service Village," in Wardha, which became his home for the rest of his life. He chose the location because of its extreme poverty and because this region was inhabited almost entirely by untouchables. He hoped it would be a place of solitude. Instead, it quickly became a pilgrimage site, and tens of thousands of people visited the village over the years. His home was a small mud-and-bamboo hut that contained a spinning wheel, a straw mat, a low writing table, and two shelves for a few books. He rose for prayer at 4:00 a.m. every morning and ate only fruit, nuts, and vegetables. As before, he and his friends made their own clothes, grew their own food, ran their own school, published their own newspapers, raised funds for the poorest of the poor, and shared everything in common. Once when he was beginning a prison term, he was told to list his occupation and wrote "farmer and weaver." Though a lawyer, politician, and journalist, Gandhi saw himself as a simple, poor man of the people, living in solitude and poverty, devoted to his friends and the struggle for peace and justice.

As the world rushed again to war, Gandhi continued to advocate nonviolence and peaceful alternatives to war. When the war began in 1939, Gandhi broke down and wept. Though he opposed the Nazis, he also opposed warfare and spoke out against it everywhere, pleading for nonviolent resistance to Hitler. His was one of the few voices in the world against World War II. In 1940, Gandhi left the Congress Party when it decided to support Britain in the war. He rejoined the following year after Churchill rejected the Congress Party's offer to help fight the Nazis. Gandhi announced repeatedly that if the Allies truly stood for the cause of democracy, they must immediately grant independence to India. His public stand against the war threatened Britain even more than his work for independence, and the British government, led by Churchill, hated Gandhi more than ever.

On August 8, 1942, Gandhi called for a new civil disobedience campaign against British rule. The next day, the British arrested him and his wife. Riots broke out throughout the country. In early 1943, Gandhi undertook a twenty-one-day fast against both British imperialism and Indian violence. He barely survived.

On February 22, 1944, Gandhi's beloved wife, Kasturbai, died in his arms in prison, after a long illness. They had been married for sixty-two years. Gandhi buried her ashes on the prison grounds. A few months before, Gandhi's secretary, one of his closest friends, had also died in prison. That spring, after Gandhi contracted malaria and nearly died, the British released him — on May 6, 1944. Altogether, Gandhi was arrested on twelve occasions during his life and spent nearly six years behind bars (2,089 days in Indian prisons and 249 days in South African prisons).

As the war came to an end and it became increasingly clear that the British would withdraw from India, Muslim politicians demanded that India be divided along religious lines to create East and West Pakistan. Hostility and riots between Hindus and Muslims broke out across the country. Gandhi decided to journey to one of the poorest regions of India, where the most brutal riots and massacres were occurring, in a living plea for unity and nonviolence. For nearly six months, Gandhi walked through Noakhali, one of the most inaccessible regions of India, made up of two and half million Muslims living and dying in desperate, absolute poverty. Though he was relatively unknown in this remote province, where no one heard any news from the outside world, within weeks the region celebrated the presence of a mahatma walking barefoot through their villages preaching nonviolence and religious unity. Gandhi would stay overnight with the first peasant who offered to take him in. Altogether, he visited forty-nine villages. He inspired the Muslims to welcome back the Hindus who had fled the region. Within a few months, the entire region was disarmed and at peace. Later, after his death, Gandhi's associates described the months in Noakhali as the most miraculous period of Gandhi's life. He walked unarmed as a pilgrim of peace into a chaotic war zone, an apostle of nonviolence in a land possessed by violence. Everyone was captivated by Gandhi. He was seventy-eight years old at the time.

As the war ended, the United States dropped atomic bombs on Hiroshima and Nagasaki, incinerating over 140,000 people in two brief flashes. Gandhi condemned the atomic bomb and pleaded with the world powers not to use these weapons again. He was the most prominent religious voice in the world against the U.S. development of nuclear weapons. He pleaded with his own country never to manufacture or use such weapons. Until the very afternoon of his death, he said repeatedly that the possession of nuclear weapons risks the destruction of the planet. His plea for nuclear disarmament became his central spiritual message until his death.

After Churchill was defeated, the new British government decided to grant independence to India and accepted Muslim demands for the creation of the separate Muslim nations of Pakistan and East Pakistan (now Bangladesh). On August 15, 1947, independence was granted. Gandhi spent the day alone in solitude, prayer, and fasting for unity and nonviolence. But as millions of Muslim refugees fled to the two Pakistans and millions of Hindus fled East and West Pakistan for India, the country exploded in violence. Hundreds of thousands of people were massacred within a few short months.

Gandhi searched for a way to stop the killing. He decided to move into a poor Muslim home in Calcutta, the scene of the worst violence, and declared a fast unto death until the violence stopped. Within seventy-three hours, Hindus and Muslims not only stopped the violence, but began to march and pray together by the thousands. As Gandhi approached death, Calcutta came to a standstill and everyone prayed for peace. Gandhi ended his fast. The violence had stopped because no one wanted him to suffer for what they were doing. Gandhi had performed another miracle. Nevertheless, during those terrible years, nearly one million Indians were killed as the country was divided.

Gandhi then moved to Delhi to try to stop the riots there. On January 13, 1948, Gandhi began another fast to the death. This was his eleventh public fast. Huge parades were organized and meetings between local politicians and religious leaders were held, and on the sixth day, fifty leading Muslims, Hindus, and Sikhs signed a peace pledge in Gandhi's presence. But Gandhi said this was not enough and broke down sobbing. They insisted their commitment to Hindu-Muslim unity was sincere. As he listened to their pleas, he decided to end his fast. The next day, on January 20, a bomb exploded while he was holding his outdoor evening prayer meeting. While many Muslims hated him as a Hindu leader, many Hindu fanatics hated him for defending and protecting Muslims. On January 29, he said to a friend, "If someone were to end my life by putting a bullet through me, and I met his bullet without a groan and breathed my last taking God's name, then alone would I have made good my claim." Gandhi expected he would be killed.

Gandhi felt that he had failed to convince India that nonviolence was the only way to independence. The partition of the country, the massacres, the riots, the deep hatreds, and the world war left him sad and depressed. Still, he continued his public work of disarmament and planned to travel to Pakistan. On January 30, 1948, at 5:10 p.m., as he walked through the garden to his evening prayer service, Gandhi was shot and killed. He fell to the ground calling out God's name.

"I have nothing new to teach the world," Gandhi wrote shortly before his death. "Truth and nonviolence are as old as the hills. All I have done is to try experiments in both on as vast a scale as I could. In doing so, I have sometimes erred and learned by my errors. Life and its problems have thus become to me so many experiments in the practice of truth and nonviolence."

Gandhi as a Spiritual Teacher and Religious Leader

"I am not a saint who has strayed into politics," Gandhi once wrote. "I am a politician who is trying to become a saint." While Adolf Hitler organized genocide in Europe, Franklin Roosevelt militarized America, Winston Churchill cheered on the Allies, and Harry Truman ordered that atomic bombs be dropped on Hiroshima and Nagasaki, Gandhi was attempting an entirely new kind of politics based on the transformative spirituality of nonviolence.

Gandhi wanted independence for his people, but he did not want to kill anyone for it. He wanted the basic human rights of food, clothing, shelter, education, jobs, health care, and dignity for the hundreds of millions of impoverished Indians. But he called for justice by first living in radical solidarity with the poorest of the poor. He demonstrated in his daily life, through the use of the spinning wheel and communal living, how they could transform their own lives, even as they sought political independence. He wanted to stop oppression everywhere in the world, but he did not want to use the methods of the oppressors and in the process become just another imperialist. He wanted to reach the heights of sanctity in his own life, and so he disciplined himself ruthlessly, denied himself basic pleasures, and shared his mistakes and faults with the world. He also refused to give in to a narrow worldview, and instead led daily interreligious prayer services, called for religious unity, and opposed any injustice committed in the name of God.

The tie that binds Gandhi's life together is that he tried to be a person of integrity and authenticity. He wanted to do God's will, and he did not want to be a hypocrite. That meant he had to identify as radically as possible with the poorest people on the face of the earth. If he wanted to achieve the heights of divinity, he said to himself, he had to touch the bottom of humanity and become one with the starving millions. He learned quickly that the path to God required the ongoing purification of his own heart and life. Throughout fifty years of letter-writing, he always maintained that the way to peace, justice, and salvation begins first with the purification of one's own heart and daily life. As he purified his inner life, he stepped deeper into public turmoil and willingly suffered for his political beliefs, undergoing repeated arrests, trials, imprisonments, death threats, attempts on his life, constant verbal abuse, and fasting for his causes, coming to the brink of death on several occasions. Never had such religious idealism been practiced politically and socially on the world stage.

When Gandhi began his personal transformation at the turn of the century in South Africa, he realized that he could never hurt or kill another human being, or indeed any creature; that there was no cause, however noble it may appear, that justified the taking of another life. At the same time, he knew he could not be passive or indifferent in the face of the violence, racism, poverty, and war. Gandhi thought that an honest spiritual search for God must thrust a person into the world in search of justice for the poor and peace between warring peoples. But he also quickly concluded that the only way to pursue social change and justice for the poor — in the name of God — was through strictly nonviolent means.

"I am endeavoring to see God through the service of humanity, for I know that God is neither in heaven, nor down below, but in every one," Gandhi wrote to a friend on August 4, 1927. If God is in everyone, Gandhi believed, then he would have to love everyone, even his enemy. He would have to side with the most oppressed, impoverished, suffering people on the planet, and not just once, but every day and for the rest of his life, come what may. If he remained true to this hard road, he knew his outcome was assured: not only political independence and peace, but the vision of God.

In this spiritual search, Gandhi came up with the method of satyagraha as a holy strategy for social and political revolution and widespread structural change. If one were willing to suffer and die for justice and peace, Gandhi taught, without even the desire to retaliate or kill, then the spirit of all-encompassing redemptive love would capture even God's attention, win the sympathy of the world, and wear down the opponent in the process until justice and freedom were achieved. It is a foolproof method, he insisted. As Gandhi sought the spiritual roots of political struggle, he realized more and more that he was merely applying the ancient spiritual teachings of Jesus, Buddha, and other religious figures to today's political crises. His great achievement was the scientific, systematic, steadfast application of ancient spiritual truths to widespread national and international problems.

"Every act has its spiritual, economic, and social implications," Gandhi told Ronald Duncan during his visit to Wardha. "The spirit is not separate. It cannot be." Gandhi saw everything he did as a religious act. "I believe God is always near me," he wrote a friend in 1906. "God is never away from me. May you also act in this faith. Believe that God is near you and always follow the truth." To understand Gandhi, we need to notice his daily dedication to prayer, meditation, and scripture study. When he was a child, Gandhi's nurse taught him whenever he was scared to repeat God's name over and over again throughout the day. He tried to continue this practice every day for the rest of his life. He sought to experience the presence of God every minute of his life. This personal spiritual search, coupled with his dramatic public search for God's nonviolent transformation of the world, inspires us today to attempt the same spiritual journey in our own lives.

"I have grown disillusioned with Western civilization," Gandhi said after returning from the Round Table conference in London. "The people that you meet on the way seem half-crazy. They spend their days in luxury or in making a bare living and retire at night thoroughly exhausted. In this state of affairs, I cannot understand when they can devote themselves to prayers."

Prayer was critically important for Gandhi. Each morning, he spent one hour in silent meditation before sunrise. Each evening, he spent another hour in silent meditation. Every day for nearly fifty years, he read from the Sermon on the Mount, the Koran, and most importantly, the Bhagavad Gita, with a focus on the second chapter, which calls for renunciation of selfishness. There he found instruction on how to do God's will and "see God face to face."

Gandhi viewed the Hindu scripture as a radical call to complete renunciation, steadfast love, and perfect nonviolence. He wrote many commentaries on the Gita, translated it several times, and tried to change his life and habits to fit its teachings. Using the teachings of the Gita, he summed up the model human being as one

> who is jealous of none; who is a fount of mercy; who is without egotism; who is selfless; who treats alike cold and heat, happiness and misery; who is ever forgiving; who is always contented; whose resolutions are firm; who has dedicated mind and soul to God; who causes no dread; who is not afraid of others; who is free from exultation, sorrow, and fear; who is pure; who is versed in action yet remains unaffected by it; who renounces all fruit, good or bad; who treats friend and foe alike; who is untouched by respect or disrespect; who is not puffed up by praise; who does not go under when people speak ill of him; who loves silence and solitude; and who has a disciplined reason.

Gandhi spent his days trying to incarnate this spiritual ideal.

Gandhi then was not just a lawyer, politician, activist, social reformer, or revolutionary: Gandhi was a contemplative, a person of God, a saint. He showed the possibilities not just of Hinduism and Christianity in practice, but what it means to be human. He did so because he relied on God. He allowed God to disarm his heart and in the process became an instrument for God's disarmament of the world. Indeed, he not only rediscovered the possibilities of peace and justice; he recovered the possibilities of holiness, innocence, and Godliness. That is why his life and martyrdom have become so influential not just for Indians, but for all people. He inspires us to seek God, to promote peace, to walk with the poor, to pursue justice, to meditate, and to speak the truth.

Gandhi's Message of Nonviolence

Gandhi's greatest contribution to humanity is his message of nonviolence as the way to peace, justice, and God. Gandhi took seriously the biblical commandments "Thou shalt not kill" and "Love your enemies," along with the Hindu tradition of *ahimsa* (nonkilling), and applied this renunciation of violence to his own heart and life as well as to South Africa, India, and the world. But he taught that nonviolence is not just refusal to kill: it is the action of love and truth as a force for positive social change. Indeed, he insisted that nonviolence was the most active and powerful force in the world. Since he saw it as the force of God, the method of God, the power of God at work for good among the human race, he concluded that nonviolence is more powerful than nuclear weapons. If millions of ordinary Americans would practice nonviolence, would peacefully, publicly, and actively resist the production and maintenance of nuclear weapons, disarmament would be assured. Nonviolence always works, he said, because it uses the method of suffering love to melt the human heart.

While Gandhi was a brilliant political strategist and revolutionary, what set him apart from others was his unique reliance upon God in his public practice of nonviolence. Nonviolence for Gandhi was not just a tactic, but a spirituality, a way of life, the center of his religion. "Nonviolence succeeds only when we have a real living faith in God," Gandhi insisted. As such, Gandhi stands on the world stage as a prophet and an apostle, a messenger from God telling us that God is nonviolent and wants us to become nonviolent even on the political, national, and international levels, if we only dare try.

Though few nations have disarmed, Gandhi's life and teaching offers an ideal that many uphold. From grassroots activists to Nobel Laureates, billions of people around the world know about Gandhi and have been touched by him. Dorothy Day, Nelson Mandela, the Dalai Lama, and Archbishop Tutu have all expressed their debt to Gandhi. Recently, while visiting the Rock and Roll Hall of Fame in Cleveland, I saw a video of the late John Lennon, at the height of his fame as a Beatle, explaining how he thought Gandhi was right and that Gandhi's way of nonviolence was the only option for himself and for humanity.

Trappist monk Thomas Merton wrote about Gandhi and edited a book of Gandhi's writings on nonviolence to help the growing peace movement oppose nuclear weapons, racism, and the war in Vietnam. Merton concluded that the key to understanding Gandhi was to grasp his nonviolence not just as a tactic, but as a spiritual path to personal, social, and global transformation. "Gandhi's spirit of nonviolence sprang from an inner realization of spiritual unity in himself," Merton wrote. "The whole Gandhian concept of nonviolent action and satyagraha is incomprehensible if it is thought to be a means of achieving unity rather than as the fruit of inner unity already achieved." If we can experience this same inner spiritual transformation, Merton declared, the power of God's spirit can work through us to transform the world.

Gandhi never gave up hope that the world would adopt his method of nonviolence. Indeed, he thought the experiment with widespread nonviolence was just beginning, that we were embarking on a whole new era in human relations, that the future of the world has the potential to be entirely different, with no more wars, no more weapons, no more racism, no more sexism, no more violence, and no more injustice. As the nightmare of World War II exploded, he told the great African American minister Howard Thurman that the only way nonviolence might be vindicated would be through an African American struggling for civil rights. In a few short years, Martin Luther King Jr. was studying Gandhi at Morehouse College, Crozier Seminary, and Boston University and would emerge to teach the West the wisdom of this great peacemaker from the East.

"As I delved deeper into the philosophy of Gandhi," King wrote in his first book, *Stride toward Freedom*,

> my skepticism concerning the power of love gradually diminished, and I came to see for the first time its potency in the area of social reform. Prior to reading Gandhi, I had about concluded that the ethics of Jesus were only effective in individual relationship. The "turn the other cheek" philosophy and the "love your enemies" philosophy were only valid, I felt, when individuals were in conflict with other individuals; when racial groups and nations were in conflict a more realistic approach seemed necessary. But after reading Gandhi, I saw how utterly mistaken I was. Gandhi

was probably the first person in history to lift the love ethic of Jesus above mere interaction between individuals to a powerful and effective social force on a large scale. For Gandhi, love was a potent instrument for social and collective transformation. It was in this Gandhian emphasis on love and nonviolence that I discovered the method for social reform that I had been seeking. I came to feel that this was the only morally and practically sound method open to oppressed people in their struggle for freedom.

I had come to see that the Christian doctrine of love operating through the Gandhian method of nonviolence was one of the most potent weapons available to African-Americans in the struggle for freedom. Christ furnished the spirit and the motivation while Gandhi furnished the method.

Gandhi's Contribution to Modern Spirituality

"If humanity is to progress," King concluded, "Gandhi is inescapable. We may ignore him at our own risk." Gandhi's contributions to modern spirituality include not only his impact on social movements around the world through the political strategy of active nonviolence and satyagraha, but his transforming influence on religion itself. Thanks to Gandhi, many of the world's religions have been inspired to return to their root beliefs of truth and nonviolence that they all share in common.

Gandhi's influence is so great and yet so sublime that it is hard to categorize his many contributions and achievements. But a few essential teachings can be gleaned from his life work and testimony.

Gandhi's primary contribution to spirituality and the world itself is nonviolence. Gandhi insisted that if our worship of God is honest, if our faith is sincere, if we want to be people of prayer, indeed, if we want to be fully human, we need to become people of nonviolence. Gandhi worshiped the God of nonviolence and announced that every major religion was rooted in nonviolence. He taught that nonviolence could be put into practice at every level of human life, in our own hearts, among our own fam-

ily and friends, in our local communities, as well as nationally
and internationally. Gandhi urges us to get rid of our guns and
bombs, stop hurting those around us, simplify our lifestyles, enter
the public struggle for disarmament and justice, and pursue the
depths of nonviolence. He said that each of us can do it, from the
poorest prisoner to presidents and popes.

More than that, Gandhi challenges people of faith to recognize the hypocrisy in their lives. He argued that we cannot go to
church, synagogue, and mosque one day, and the next day sanction war, support executions, foster racism, or pay for nuclear
weapons. We cannot claim to be people of faith and Godliness
and at the same time, contribute to the world's faithlessness and
godlessness, as seen in murder, executions, warfare, and nuclear
weapons. For Gandhi, the only authentic spirituality is a spirituality of nonviolence. Every facet of life from now on, he said,
had to be gauged from the perspective of nonviolence. When he
applied this spirituality of nonviolence to South Africa and India,
he showed how we can transform politics, religion, social institutions, laws, and even empires. He knew it would work because
nonviolence, he said, is the way of God.

Through his dedication and sacrifice, Gandhi unlocked the
spiritual dynamite, not only in the Hindu scriptures, but in the
Gospels as never before, just when the world needed it most,
at the dawn of the nuclear age. He gave us a way out of our
madness. In particular, he showed Christians that the pinnacle
of Jesus' teaching, the Sermon on the Mount, was not impractical, that it could be applied to nations as well as individuals,
that it was not an interim ethic but the hallmark of all ethics. For
Gandhi, the Sermon on the Mount was nothing less than a clar-
ion call to active nonviolence, in Jesus' words, not to offer violent
resistance to evil but to love one's enemies. Indeed, Gandhi held
that Jesus was the greatest practitioner of active nonviolence in
history, from his teachings and actions to his martyrdom on
the cross. He said the only people in the whole world who do
not understand, much less accept, the nonviolence of Jesus are
Christians.

Gandhi's influence on Christianity is particularly important.

He proclaimed that to be a Christian one has to practice nonviolence. Anything less is not just infidelity, but betrayal. From now on, he pointed out, instead of being a pawn to state-sanctioned violence, like Judas handing Jesus over to the empire, or practicing justified, redemptive violence, like Peter chopping off a soldier's ear in self-defense, Christians need to take seriously Jesus' last words to the community, "Put away the sword." In light of Gandhi's critique, every Christian church, by definition, has to become a community of nonviolence.

Second, "noncooperation with evil is as much a duty as cooperation with good," Gandhi said during the Great Trial of 1922. If we want to work for peace and live in peace, we must, due to the nature of the world, also work against war and stand against war. We need to be publicly active in promoting the common good as well as organizing against the common evil. Most people of faith have yet to grasp this essential spiritual insight.

Third, Gandhi thought that faith pushes us to promote peace and justice, but he revived the deep wisdom held by every ancient religious tradition that the way to positive, nonviolent social change for peace is through risk and sacrifice. Gandhi insisted that these issues are a matter of life and death, that they are spiritual questions, and that peace and justice require lifelong dedication and the willingness to suffer and die. This is not a new teaching. Jesus commanded his followers to take up the cross. The early Christians wrote that the way to the reign of God lay in our participation in the Paschal Mystery, the cross and resurrection. Gandhi translated the cross to mean an active willingness to be arrested, tried, imprisoned, and killed for the cause of justice and peace. His path to political transformation is fundamentally rooted in the spiritual requirement of risk, renunciation, sacrifice, even martyrdom.

Fourth, Gandhi teaches us to accept suffering, even to court suffering, if we want personal transformation, political revolution, and a vision of God. "Nonviolence in its dynamic condition means conscious suffering," Gandhi wrote. "It does not mean meek submission to the will of the evildoer, but it means the pitting of one's whole soul against the will of the tyrant. Working under this law of our being, it is possible for a single individual to defy the whole might of an unjust empire to save his honor, his religion, his soul and lay the foundation for that empire's fall or regeneration." Indeed, Gandhi said that the soul of peacemaking lay not in the art of killing, but in the art of voluntary suffering and dying. He taught, like Jesus, that we must constantly die to ourselves and confront systemic injustice with a profound willingness to lose our freedom and our lives if necessary, in order to be true to God's reign of nonviolence.

When asked to sum up the meaning of life in three words or less, Gandhi responded cheerfully, "That's easy: Renounce and enjoy." Today, it is not popular to talk about self-denial or voluntary suffering, but Gandhi talked about it all the time. The key to his daring achievements lies in his own ongoing suffering, including his poverty, celibacy, arrests, imprisonments, attacks, and assassination. He testified throughout his life that the more he denied himself and sought God and the good of humanity, no matter what the personal cost to him, the greater the joy and peace he experienced within himself.

Fifth, though Gandhi was a lawyer, politician, and revolutionary, he acknowledged that his most powerful weapon was prayer. Through his daily meditation, he came to believe in the presence and nearness of God in day-to-day life. He did not see visions or hear voices, but his prayer led him to a near total reliance on God that gave him the faith (much more important than courage) to undertake his bold public actions for justice and independence. Because Gandhi practiced peace through prayer and mindfulness, he was neither angry or strident. He radiated peace. He laughed constantly. He was full of joy. The more influential his life became, the more he relied on prayer, seeking greater solitude, even taking one day a week in total silence for the last two decades of his life. His commitment to prayer and his devotion to the spirit working in his heart through prayer transformed Gandhi from a politician into a saint, someone who does God's will, through whom God speaks and moves and touches the human race.

Sixth, Gandhi held that radical purity of heart bears enormous positive ramifications for the entire world. This message was one of the most shocking and consistent core beliefs I discovered as I read through his collected works. He firmly believed that the more we purify our inner lives, the more our lives will serve God's work to end war, poverty, and injustice. He taught that personal integrity is necessary for an authentic spirituality, for nonviolence. To this end, he suggested regular fasting throughout one's life and became an advocate and proponent of fasting as a way to repent of one's personal sins and the sins of those we love. He would tell all politicians, activists, and religious leaders to get their own hearts in order, to let God disarm their hearts, if they wanted to be of any help to others.

Seventh, Gandhi practiced a living solidarity with the poor and oppressed. Long before liberation theology, Gandhi gave away his money and personal possessions, renounced his career, moved to a communal farm, made his own clothes, dressed like the poorest Indian peasants, and shared their meager diet of fruits and vegetables. His willingness to go to jail and his defense of the untouchables were other ways to share in the poverty of the masses. "Self-realization I hold to be impossible without service of and identification with the poorest," Gandhi wrote. If we want to find God, he said, we must go to the poor, walk with them, serve the poor, learn from them, be disarmed by them, and become one with them. The poor will teach us the truth, show us God, and share God's reign with us. Gandhi's solidarity with the poor echoes the Beatitudes and Jesus' own unity with "the least," as outlined in the Gospel of Matthew, chapter 25. Ask yourself if the next step you contemplate, Gandhi taught a friend, is of any use to the poorest person on the planet. Do whatever is most helpful for that person, and you will do God's will.

Eighth, Gandhi advocated powerlessness as the path to God. Though he mingled with kings and viceroys and was hailed as the father of India, he preferred the company of the poor and urged everyone to avoid attaining power over others. "Have nothing to do with power," he told journalist Vincent Sheean a few days before being assassinated. Gandhi believed that people of faith and nonviolence should not hold any position of authority over others because domination and the nation-state systems are rooted in violence. He himself could easily have become the first president of India, but he chose instead the path of downward mobility. He saw how power corrupts and blinds even the best people. He realized too that it sets us against the God of the poor. Since he sincerely wanted to do God's will most of all, he knew he had to seek the powerlessness of the poor, just as Jesus did. If we all tried to become powerless, instead of powerful, he taught, we would discover our common identity as equal sisters and brothers of one another, and begin to serve one another. Then, peace would grow among us.

Ninth, Gandhi taught that each of the world's religions has a piece of the truth and deserves our respect. By advocating tolerance and the equality of religions, Gandhi suggested that we all share the same common ground of nonviolence and can live at peace with one another, even while holding different faiths. With this basic wisdom, Gandhi paved a new path to peace. He understood that most wars and injustice have religious roots in ethnic hatred, pride, and idolatry. Just as the violence he witnessed in India was based in religious division and hatred, so will future wars be rooted in division and ethnic hatred. The remedy is simple: our peacemaking efforts must begin with interreligious dialogue and cooperation, regionally and nationally. This will not only hasten the coming of peace, but model the peace we seek. This new interfaith peacemaking becomes possible when people of different faiths discover the common ground of nonviolence in all faiths.

Tenth, Gandhi held that the spiritual life, as well as all political and social work, requires a fearless pursuit of truth. Indeed, he consistently said that he worshiped God not just as the God of nonviolence, but as the God of truth. He came to the startling conclusion, as a devout Hindu, that Truth is God. In this journey, he demonstrated that power of John's Gospel declaration that "the truth shall set you free." Over and over again he spoke the truth publicly, fearlessly, openly, and in total disregard of the consequences. He told the truth about poverty, war, racism, imperialism, and nuclear weapons when few could barely imagine it, much less speak it. Gandhi's spirituality was not rooted in any feel-good, warm-fuzzy, New Age false piety. It was based in truth and spoken openly with love. Rarely has any public figure spoken as boldly as Gandhi did. He knew that if he clung to the truth, he was clinging to God and that the truth once proclaimed would do its own work and lead to new freedom and peace.

Eleventh, Gandhi urged that we let go of results and simply trust in the goodness of the struggle for peace itself. Renunciation of results was a hallmark of the Bhagavad Gita and became the centerpiece of Gandhi's personal theology. Every day he reflected on this spiritual requirement, and over time grew freer from the compulsion of having to be successful or effective, even though he worked hard to change the world. "Our task is to work away on behalf of what we consider to be right and just," he said, "and to leave the result to God, without whose permission or knowledge not a blade of grass moves." This spiritual path is particularly challenging for Americans, socialized as we are in a culture that idolizes success, achievement, and effectiveness. But Gandhi's own life exemplifies the teaching: the more he pursued the truth of justice and peace through active nonviolence and the more he let go of his desire to achieve these goals and placed the results in God's hands, the more that happened in his life. Here lies one of the mysteries of the spiritual life: the more we give ourselves to the struggle but give the results to God, the more good fruit of peace and justice we receive as a gift from God. God was able to do more through him, Gandhi said, the more he left the outcome in God's hands.

Twelfth, Gandhi understood these basic principles of truth and nonviolence not just as romantic ideals or pious platitudes, but as actual laws of the universe, with the same palpable hold as the law of gravity. If we pursue truth and nonviolence, our lives will bear the good fruit of truth and nonviolence, Gandhi said. But he added that this outcome was as sure as Newton's discovery, that if we let go of an apple, it will in fact fall to the ground. Similarly, he observed, violence can only lead to further violence. Violence is not only immoral; it is always impractical. With this insight, Gandhi teaches that there are no just wars, just revolutions, justified executions, or justified weapons of deterrence. Likewise, every action rooted in prayerful, peaceful, loving, committed nonviolence will bear good fruit. Again, he was simply explaining the Sermon on the Mount: you shall reap what you sow.

"Whether humanity will consciously follow the law of love, I do not know," Gandhi wrote. "But that need not disturb me. The law will work just as the law of gravitation works, whether we accept it or not. The person who discovered the law of love was a far greater scientist than any of our modern scientists. Only our explorations have not gone far enough and so it is not possible for everyone to see all its workings."

Gandhi's Writings

"My writings should be cremated with my body," Gandhi once wrote. "What I have done will endure, not what I have said or written." Happily, the government of India disregarded his advice and spent over twenty years collecting every statement, letter, and word written by Gandhi, in one of the most exhaustive publishing projects ever undertaken. In 1984, India completed the publication of the ninety-five volumes of *The Collected Works of Mahatma Gandhi,* a massive undertaking with over forty-three thousand pages of letters, speeches, essays, telegrams, memos, and books by Gandhi himself, every piece of writing they could find. (There are probably thousands of letters scattered around the world still to be added.)

Gandhi's writings comprise one of the largest collections by a spiritual and political figure ever gathered. For this book, I read through those ninety-five volumes, as well as dozens of other collections and biographies. It has been an exhausting, eye-opening, and inspiring experience. But any effort to distill all that material into a slim volume of essential writings will be incomplete. For further study, I recommend reading Louis Fischer's outstanding definitive biography, *The Life of Mahatma Gandhi;* Thomas Merton's own collection, *Gandhi on Nonviolence;* and the recently published biography by Stanley Wolpert entitled *Gandhi's Passion.*

Gandhi was not quite a literary figure, like Thomas Merton; or a theologian, like Karl Rahner; or an intellectual, like Simone Weil; or a poet, like Thich Nhat Hanh and Daniel Berrigan. He was a man of action, and though he wrote for hours every day, it was always in haste, as a duty — to urge others on to the spiritual life and political work of nonviolence. So his writings should be considered in the context of a life in turmoil.

I have broken down Gandhi's writings into a few key groupings, beginning with his autobiographical writings and followed by sections on "The Search for God," "The Pursuit of Truth," "The Practice of Nonviolence," "The Discipline of Prayer and Fasting," "The Urgent Need for Nuclear Disarmament," and "The Life of Steadfast Resistance," which features several key speeches and a sampling of his letters. All quotations are from *The Collected Works of Mahatma Gandhi*, vols. 1–95 (Ahmedabad: Navajivan Trust, 1967–84), unless otherwise noted. Instead of listing the page numbers from *The Collected Works*, I have simply listed the volume and date. Also, I have applied Gandhi's feminism to his writing and in some cases changed the text to inclusive language.

Conclusion

In the end, Gandhi challenges each of us to seek God through our own active pursuit of truth and nonviolence. He invites us to pursue the spiritual, political, economic, and social depths of peace with the same fierce determination and sacrifice that he undertook. Gandhi urges us to let go of our desire for fame, fortune, power, and ego, and instead to walk with the poor, simplify our lives, pray to God each day, practice nonviolence in every area of our life, and work publicly for the abolition of nuclear weapons, war, poverty, racism, sexism, hunger, the death penalty, abortion, the sanctions on Iraq, handguns, environmental destruction, homelessness, religious bigotry, animal exploitation, and violence of any kind. He calls for nothing less than the total transformation of our lives and our world. In this call, he stands with

Francis of Assisi and Dorothy Day as a messenger of God and a model of faith and peace.

After the September 11, 2001, attacks, Gandhi's spirituality, teachings, and example are more relevant to us than ever. During those difficult months in late 2001, I worked as a chaplain with thousands of grieving families and rescue workers in New York City, while also speaking out around the country against the perils of retaliatory violence. I often wondered what Gandhi would say and do, but I know he would call us to creative nonviolent alternatives. He would insist that violence only sows the seeds of violence, and that we should break the cycle of violence, terrorism, and war by sowing the seeds of nonviolence. He would challenge us to address the roots of terrorism, eliminate poverty and nuclear weapons, and embrace the whole variety of human life and religious experience. In other words, he would still insist on the spirituality of nonviolence as the source of hope and the way to peace.

"We are constantly being astonished these days at the amazing discoveries in the field of violence," Gandhi once observed. "But I maintain that far more undreamt of and seemingly impossible discoveries will be made in the field of nonviolence."

Gandhi would want anyone who reads his words to undertake similar "experiments with truth" in their own lives, in pursuit of new discoveries in the field of nonviolence, so that a new day of peace with justice will soon dawn and we can all rejoice to see God face to face. May his hope and prayer come true.

John Dear

1

My Life Is My Message:
Autobiographical Writings

A few months before he was assassinated, Mahatma Gandhi was asked to sum up his message for the world. For years, Gandhi spent one day a week in silence, no matter how many people had come to meet him. This was a day of silence, so he grabbed a pencil, wrote a few words, and passed on the paper. "My life is my message," it said.

"My life is one indivisible whole, and all my activities run into one another, and they all have their rise in my insatiable love of humanity," Gandhi wrote on another occasion. "Truth and nonviolence are as old as the hills. All I have done is to try experiments in both on as vast a scale as I could do. Life and its problems have thus become to me so many experiments in the practice of truth and nonviolence."

Gandhi wanted people not just to study his ideas, but to put them into practice in their own lives. He wanted people to pursue their own experiments in active nonviolence. In 1925, after he was released from prison and decided to pull back from his nonstop organizing, he decided to write his story. Each week a new chapter appeared in his newspaper, Young India. *He finished his autobiography in late 1928 and later published it as a book under the title,* The Story of My Experiments with Truth.

Gandhi's autobiography offers a candid record of his personal journey, from his childhood and marriage at age thirteen,

49

*to his years as a lawyer and organizer for freedom and equality
in South Africa, to his experiments with diet and health care,
and the birth of India's independence movement. From the beginning, he insists that his life has been nothing less than a daily
effort "to see God face to face."*

*"I claim to be no more than an average person with less than
average ability," Gandhi wrote in 1936. "I have not the shadow of
a doubt that anyone can achieve what I have, if that person would
make the same effort and cultivate the same hope and faith."*

*(All the following excerpts are from his autobiography, which
is located in volume 39, pages 1–402, in the* Collected Works.
*His autobiography is available in the United States from Beacon
Press [Boston, 1957].)*

TO SEE GOD FACE TO FACE

My life consists of nothing but experiments with truth. I believe,
or at any rate flatter myself with the belief, that a connected account of all these experiments will not be without benefit to the
reader. My experiments in the political field are now known, not
only to India, but to a certain extent to the "civilized" world. For
me, they have not much value; and the title of "Mahatma" that
they have won for me has, therefore, even less. Often the title has
deeply pained me; and there is not a moment I can recall when
it may be said to have tickled me. But I should certainly like to
narrate my experiments in the spiritual field which are known
only to myself, and from which I have derived such power as I
possess for working in the political field. If the experiments are
really spiritual, then there can be no room for self-praise. They
can only add to my humility. The more I reflect and look back on
the past, the more vividly do I feel my limitations.

What I want to achieve, what I have been striving and pining to achieve these thirty years, is self-realization, to see God
face to face, to attain *Moksha* [salvation]. I live and move and
have my being in pursuit of this goal. All that I do by way of
speaking and writing, and all my ventures in the political field,

are directed to this same end. But as I have all along believed that what is possible for one is possible for all, my experiments have not been conducted in the closet, but in the open, and I do not think this fact detracts from their spiritual value. There are some things which are known only to oneself and one's Maker. These are clearly incommunicable. The experiments I am about to relate are not such. But they are spiritual, or rather moral; for the essence of religion is morality.

Far be it from me to claim any degree of perfection for these experiments. I claim for them nothing more than does a scientist who, though he conducts his experiments with the utmost accuracy, forethought, and minuteness, never claims any finality about his conclusions, but keeps an open mind regarding them. I have gone through deep self-introspection, searched myself through and through, and examined and analyzed every psychological situation. Yet I am far from claiming any finality or infallibility about my conclusions.

For me, truth is the sovereign principle, which includes numerous other principles. This truth is not only truthfulness in word, but truthfulness in thought also, and not only the relative truth of our conception, but the Absolute Truth, the Eternal Principle, that is God. There are innumerable definitions of God, because God's manifestations are innumerable. They overwhelm me with wonder and awe and for a moment stun me. But I worship God as Truth only. I have not yet found God, but I am seeking after God. I am prepared to sacrifice the things dearest to me in pursuit of this quest. Even if the sacrifice demanded be my very life, I hope I may be prepared to give it. But as long as I have not realized this Absolute Truth so long must I hold by the relative truth as I have conceived it. That relative truth must, meanwhile, be my beacon, my shield and buckler. Though this path is straight and narrow and sharp as the razor's edge, for me it has been the quickest and easiest. Even my Himalayan blunders have seemed trifling to me because I have kept strictly to this path. For the path has saved me from coming to grief, and I have gone forward according to my light. Often in my progress I have had faint glimpses of the Absolute Truth, God, and daily the conviction is growing upon me that God alone is real and all else is unreal. Let those who wish, realize how the conviction has grown upon me. Let them share my experiments and share also my conviction if they can. The further conviction has been growing upon me that whatever is possible for me is possible even for a child, and I have sound reasons for saying so. The instruments of the quest of truth are as simple as they are difficult. They may appear quite impossible to an arrogant person, and quite possible to an innocent child. Seekers after truth should be humbler than the dust. The world crushes the dust under its feet, but seekers after truth should so humble themselves that even the dust could crush them. Only then, and not till then, will they have a glimpse of truth. The dialogue between Vasishtha and Vishvamitra makes this abundantly clear. Christianity and Islam also amply bear it out.

Let hundreds like me perish, but let truth prevail. Let us not reduce the standard of truth even by a hair's breadth for judging erring mortals like myself. For it is an unbroken torture to me that I am still so far from God, who as I fully know, governs every breath of my life, and whose offspring I am.

THE GITA AND
THE SERMON ON THE MOUNT

Toward the end of my second year in England I came across two Theosophists, brothers and both unmarried. They talked to me about the Bhagavad Gita. They were reading Sir Edwin Arnold's translation, *The Song Celestial,* and they invited me to read the original with them. I felt ashamed, as I had read the divine poem neither in Sanskrit nor in Gujarati. I was constrained to tell them that I had not read the Gita, but that I would gladly read it with them, and that though my knowledge of Sanskrit was meager, still I hoped to be able to understand the original to the extent of telling where the translation failed to bring out the meaning. I began reading the Gita with them. The verses in the second chapter

If one
Ponders on objects of the sense, there springs
Attraction; from attraction grows desire,
Desire flames to fierce passion, passion breeds
Recklessness; then the memory — all betrayed —
Lets noble purpose go, and saps the mind,
Till purpose, mind, and humanity are all undone

made a deep impression on my mind, and they still ring in my ears. The book struck me as one of priceless worth. The impression has ever since been growing on me with the result that I regard it today as the book par excellence for the knowledge of Truth. It has afforded me invaluable help in my moments of gloom. It was only after some years that it became a book of daily reading.

I recall having read, at the brothers' instance, Madame Blavatsky's *Key to Theosophy*. This book stimulated in me the desire to read books on Hinduism, and disabused me of the notion fostered by the missionaries that Hinduism was rife with superstition.

About the same time I met a good Christian from Manchester in a vegetarian boarding house. He talked to me about Christianity. He said, "I am a vegetarian. I do not drink. Many Christians are meat-eaters and drink, no doubt; but neither meat-eating nor drinking is enjoined by scripture. Do please read the Bible." I accepted his advice, and he got me a copy. I have a faint recollection that he himself used to sell copies of the Bible, and I purchased from him an edition containing maps, concordance, and other aids. I began reading it, but I could not possibly read through the Old Testament. I read the book of Genesis, and the chapters that followed invariably sent me to sleep. But just for the sake of being able to say that I had read it, I plodded through the other books with much difficulty and without the least interest or understanding. I disliked reading the book of Numbers.

But the New Testament produced a different impression, especially the Sermon on the Mount, which went straight to my heart. I compared it with the Bhagavad Gita. The verses, "But I say to you, do not [violently] resist evil: whoever shall strike you on the right cheek, turn the other cheek. And if anyone takes away your coat, let him have your cloak as well," delighted me beyond measure. My young mind tried to unify the teaching of the Gita and the Sermon on the Mount. That renunciation was the highest form of religion appealed to me greatly.

THE MOST CREATIVE EXPERIENCE
OF MY LIFE

On the seventh or eighth day after my arrival in South Africa, I left Durban. A first-class seat was booked for me. It was usual there to pay five shillings extra, if one needed a bedding. Abdulla Sheth insisted that I should book one bedding but, out of obstinacy and pride and with a view to saving five shillings, I declined. Abdulla Sheth warned me. "Look now," he said, "this is a different country from India. Thank God, we have enough and to spare. Please do not stint yourself in anything that you may need."

I thanked him and asked him not to be anxious.

The train reach Maritzburg, the capital of Natal, at about 9 p.m. Beddings used to be provided at this station. A railway servant came and asked me if I wanted one. "No," I said, "I have one with me." He went away. But a passenger came next and looked me up and down. He saw that I was a "colored" man. This disturbed him. Out he went and came in again with one or two officials. They all kept quiet, when another official came to me and said, "Come along, you must go to the van compartment."

"But I have a first-class ticket," I said.

"That doesn't matter," the other rejoined. "I tell you, you must go to the van compartment."

"I tell you, I was permitted to travel in this compartment at Durban, and I insist on going on in it."

"No, you won't," said the official. "You must leave this compartment, or else I shall have to call a police constable to push you out."

"Yes, you may. I refuse to get out voluntarily."

The constable came. He took me by the hand and pushed me out. My luggage was also taken out. I refused to go to the other compartment and the train steamed away. I went and sat in the waiting room, keeping my handbag with me, and leaving the other luggage where it was. The railway authorities had taken charge of it.

It was winter, and winter in the higher regions of South Africa is severely cold. Maritzburg being at a high altitude, the cold was extremely bitter. My overcoat was in my luggage, but I did not dare to ask for it lest I should be insulted again, so I sat and shivered. There was no light in the room. A passenger came in at about midnight and possibly wanted to talk to me. But I was in no mood to talk.

I began to think of my duty. Should I fight for my rights or go back to India, or should I go on to Pretoria without minding the insults, and return to India after finishing the case? It would be cowardice to run back to India without fulfilling my obligation. The hardship to which I was subjected was superficial — only a symptom of the deep disease of color prejudice. I should try, if possible, to root out the disease and suffer hardships in the process. Redress for wrongs I should seek only to the extent that would be necessary for the removal of the color prejudice.

So I decided to take the next available train to Pretoria.

The following morning I sent a long telegram to the General Manager of the railway and also informed Abdulla Sheth, who immediately met the General Manager. The Manager justified the conduct of the railway authorities, but informed him that he had already instructed the Station Master to see that I reached my destination safely. Abdulla Sheth wired to the Indian merchants in Maritzburg and to friends in other places to meet me and look after me. The merchants came to see me at the station and tried to comfort me by narrating their own hardships and explaining that what had happened to me was nothing unusual. They also said that Indians traveling first- or second-class had to expect trouble from railway officials and white passengers. The day was thus spent in listening to these tales of woe.

THE INFINITE POSSIBILITIES
OF UNIVERSAL LOVE

If I found myself entirely absorbed in the service of the Indian community in South Africa, the reason behind it was my desire for self-realization. I had made the religion of service my own, as I felt that God could be realized only through service. And service for me was the service of India, because it came to me without my seeking, because I had an aptitude for it. I had gone to South Africa for travel, for finding an escape from Kathiawad intrigues, and for gaining my own livelihood. But as I have said, I found myself in search for God and striving for self-realization.

Christian friends had whetted my appetite for knowledge, which had become almost insatiable, and they would not leave me in peace, even if I desired to be indifferent. In Durban, Mr. Spencer Walton, the head of the South Africa General Mission, found me out. I became almost a member of his family. At the back of this acquaintance was of course my contact with Christians in Pretoria. Mr. Walton had a manner all his own. I do not recollect his ever having invited me to embrace Christianity. But he placed his life as an open book before me, and let me watch all his movements. Mrs. Walton is a very gentle and talented woman. I liked the attitude of this couple. We knew the fundamental differences between us. Any amount of discussion could not efface them. Yet even differences prove helpful, where there are tolerance, charity, and truth. I liked Mr. and Mrs. Walton's humility, perseverance, and devotion to work, and we met very frequently.

This friendship kept alive my interest in religion. It was impossible now to get the leisure that I used to have in Pretoria for my religious studies. But what little time I could spare I turned to good account. My religious correspondence continued. I read with interest Max Muller's book *India: What Can It Teach Us?*

and the translation of the *Upanishads* published by the Theo-
sophical Society. All this enhanced my regard for Hinduism, and
its beauties began to grow upon me. It did not, however, prejudice me against other religions. I read Washington Irving's *Life
of Muhammad and His Successors* and Carlyle's panegyric on the
prophet. These books raised Muhammad in my estimation. I also
read a book called *The Sayings of Zarathustra.*

Thus I gained more knowledge of the different religions. The
study stimulated my self-introspection and fostered in me the
habit of putting into practice whatever appealed to me in my
studies. Thus I began some of the Yogic practices, as well as I
could understand them from a reading of the Hindu books.

I made too an intensive study of Tolstoy's books. *The Gospels
in Brief, What to Do?* and other books made a deep impression
on me. I began to realize more and more the infinite possibilities
of universal love.

BEGINNING A LIFE
OF NONVIOLENCE

People and their deeds are two distinct things. Whereas a good
deed should call forth approbation and a wicked deed disappro-
bation, the doer of the deed, whether good or wicked, always
deserves respect or pity as the case may be. "Hate the sin and
not the sinner" is a precept which, though easy enough to understand, is rarely practiced, and that is why the poison of hatred
spreads in the world.

This nonviolence is the basis of the search for truth. I am realizing every day that the search is vain unless it is founded on
nonviolence as the basis. It is quite proper to resist and attack a
system, but to resist and attack its author is tantamount to resisting and attacking oneself. For we are all tarred with the same
brush, and are children of one and the same Creator, and as such
the divine powers within us are infinite. To slight a single human
being is to slight those divine powers, and thus to harm not only
that person but the whole world.

A variety of incidents in my life have conspired to bring me in close contact with people of many creeds and many communities, and my experience with all of them warrants the statement that I have known no distinction between relatives and strangers, compatriots and foreigners, white and colored, Hindus and Indians of other faiths, whether Muslims, Parsis, Christians, or Jews. I may say that my heart has been incapable of making any such distinctions. I cannot claim this as a special virtue, as it is in my very nature, rather than a result of any effort on my part, whereas in the case of nonviolence, celibacy, nonpossession, and other cardinal virtues, I am fully conscious of a continuous striving for their cultivation.

When I was practicing law in Durban, my office clerks often stayed with me, and there were among them Hindus and Christians, or to describe them by their provinces, Gujaratis and Tamilians. I do not recollect having ever regarded them as anything but my kith and kin. I treated them as members of my family, and had unpleasantness with my wife if ever she stood in the way of my treating them as such. One of the clerks was a Christian, born of Panchama parents.

The house was built after the Western model and the rooms rightly had no outlets for dirty water. Each room had therefore chamber-pots. Rather than have them cleaned by a servant or a sweeper, my wife or I attended to them. The clerks who made themselves completely at home would naturally clean their own pots, but the Christian clerk was a newcomer, and it was our duty to attend to his bedroom. My wife managed the pots of the others, but to clean those used by one who had been a Panchama seemed to her to be the limit, and we fell out. She could not bear the pots being cleaned by me; neither did she like doing it herself. Even today I can recall the picture of her chiding me, her eyes red with anger, and pearl drops streaming down her cheeks, as she descended the ladder, pot in hand. But I was a cruelly kind husband. I regarded myself as her teacher, and so harassed her out of my blind love for her.

I was far from being satisfied by her merely carrying the pot.

I would have her do it cheerfully. So I said, raising my voice, "I will not stand this nonsense in my house."

The words pierced her like an arrow.

She shouted back, "Keep your house to yourself and let me go." I forgot myself, and the spring of compassion dried up in me. I caught her by the hand and dragged the helpless woman to the gate, which was just opposite the ladder, and proceeded to open it with the intention of pushing her out. The tears were running down her cheeks in torrents, and she cried, "Have you no sense of shame? Must you so far forget yourself? Where am I to go? I have no parents or relatives here to harbor me. Being your wife, you think I must put up with your cuffs and kicks? For heaven's sake, behave yourself and shut the gate. Let us not be found making scenes like this!"

I put on a brave face, but was really ashamed and shut the gate. If my wife could not leave me, neither could I leave her. We have had numerous bickerings, but the end has always been peace between us. The wife, with her matchless powers of endurance, has always been the victor.

Today I am in a position to narrate the incident with some detachment, as it belongs to a period out of which I have fortunately emerged. I am no longer a blind, infatuated husband. I am no more my wife's teacher. We are tried friends, the one no longer regarding the other as the object of lust. She has been a faithful nurse throughout my illnesses, serving without any thought of reward.

The incident in question occurred in 1898, when I had no conception of celibacy. It was a time when I thought that the wife was the object of her husband's lust, born to do her husband's behest, rather than a helpmate, a comrade, and a partner in the husband's joys and sorrows.

It was in the year 1900 that these ideas underwent a radical transformation, and in 1906 they took concrete shape with a vow of chastity. Suffice it to say that with the gradual disappearance in me of the carnal appetite, my domestic life became and is becoming more and more peaceful, sweet, and happy.

BUILDING A NEW COMMUNITY IN INDIA

The Satyagraha Ashram was founded in Ahmedabad, India, on the May 25, 1915. Shraddhanandji wanted me to settle in Hardvar. Some of my Calcutta friends recommended Vaidyana-thadham. Others strongly urged me to choose Rajkot. But when I happened to pass through Ahmedabad, many friends pressed me to settle down there, and they volunteered to find the expenses of the Ashram, as well as a house for us to live in.

I had a predilection for Ahmedabad. Being a Gujarati I thought I should be able to render the greatest service to the country through the Gujarati language. And then, as Ahmedabad was an ancient center of handloom weaving, it was likely to be the most favorable field for the revival of the cottage industry of hand-spinning. There was also the hope that, the city being the capital of Gujarat, monetary help from its wealthy citizens would be more available here than elsewhere.

The question of untouchability was naturally among the subjects discussed with the Ahmedabad friends. I made it clear to them that I should take the first opportunity of admitting an untouchable candidate to the Ashram if he was otherwise worthy.

The first thing we had to settle was the name of the Ashram. I consulted friends. Among the names suggested were "Sevashram" (the Abode of Service), "Tapovan" (the Abode of Austerities), etc. I liked the name "Sevashram" but for the absence of emphasis on the method of service. "Tapovan" seemed to be a pretentious title, because we could not presume to be tapasvins, people of austerity. Our creed was devotion to truth, and our business was the search for and insistence on truth. I wanted to acquaint India with the method I had tried in South Africa, and I desired to test in India the extent to which its application might be possible. So my companions and I selected the name "Satyagraha Ashram," as conveying both our goal and our method of service.

For the conduct of the Ashram a code of rules and observances was necessary. A draft was therefore prepared and friends were invited to express their opinions on it. We were in all about twenty-five men and women. All took their meals in a common kitchen and strove to live as one family.

MY FIRST EXPERIMENT
IN NONVIOLENCE IN INDIA

Champaran is the land of King Janaka. Just as it abounds in mango groves, so it used to be full of indigo plantations until the year 1917. The Champaran tenant was bound by law to plant three out of every twenty parts of his land with indigo for his landlord. I must confess that I did not then know even the name, much less the geographical position of Champaran, and I had hardly any notion of indigo plantations. I had seen packets of indigo, but little dreamed that it was grown and manufactured in Champaran at great hardship to thousands of agriculturists.

Rajkumar Shukla was one of the farmers who had been under this harrow, and he was filled with a passion to wash away the stain of indigo for the thousands who were suffering as he had suffered. This man caught hold of me at Lucknow, where I had gone for the Congress of 1916. He wanted me personally to visit Champaran and witness the miseries of the peasants there. I told him that I would include Champaran in the tour which I had contemplated and give it a day or two.

So early in 1917, we left Calcutta for Champaran, looking just like fellow rustics. I did not even know the train. He took me to it, and we traveled together, reaching Patna in the morning.

"Having studied these cases," I said [later to the organizers], "I have come to the conclusion that we should stop going to law courts. Taking such cases to the courts does little good. Where the peasants are so crushed and fear-stricken, law courts are useless. The real relief for them is to be free from fear. We cannot sit still until we have driven the indigo system out of Bihar. I had thought that I should be able to leave here in two days, but I now realize that the work might take even two years. I am prepared to give them time, if necessary."

My object was to inquire into the condition of the Champaran

agriculturists and understand their grievances against the indigo
planters. For this purpose it was necessary that I should meet
thousands of peasants. But I deemed it essential, before starting on my inquiry, to know the planters' side of the case and
see the Commissioner of the division. I sought and was granted
appointments with both.

The Secretary of the Planters' Association told me plainly that
I was an outsider and that I had no business to come between
the planters and their tenants, but if I had any representation
to make, I might submit it in writing. I politely told him that I
did not regard myself as an outsider, and that I had every right
to inquire into the condition of the tenants if they desired me
to do so.

The Commissioner, on whom I called, proceeded to bully me,
and advised me forthwith to leave the area.

Champaran is a district of the Tirhut division and Motihari
is its headquarters. Rajkumar Shukla's place was in the vicinity
of Bettiah, and the tenants were the poorest in the district. He
wanted me to see them and I was equally anxious to do so.

So I started with my co-workers for Motihari the same day.
Babu Gorakh Prasad harbored us in his home. It could hardly
contain us all. The very same day we heard that about five miles
from Motihari, a tenant had been ill-treated. It was decided that
in company with Babu Dharanidhar Prasad, I should go and see
him the next morning, and we accordingly set off for the place
on the back of an elephant. An elephant, by the way, is about
as common in Champaran as a cart in Gujarat. We had scarcely
gone half way when a messenger from the Police Superintendent
overtook us. He served on me a notice to leave Champaran, and
drove me in his hired carriage to my place. On his asking me to
acknowledge the service of the notice, I wrote to the effect that I
did not propose to comply with it and leave Champaran till my
inquiry was finished. Thereupon I received a summons to stand
trial the next day for disobeying the order to leave Champaran.

The news of the notice and the summons spread like wildfire,
and I was told that Motihari that day witnessed unprecedented
scenes. Gorakhbabu's house and the court house overflowed with

people. Fortunately I had finished all my work during the night and so was able to cope with the crowds. My companions proved the greatest help. They occupied themselves with regulating the crowds, for the latter followed me wherever I went.

A sort of friendliness sprang up between the officials — the Collector, Magistrate, Police Superintendent — and myself. I might have legally resisted the notices served on me. Instead, I accepted them all, and my conduct toward the officials was correct. They thus saw that I did not want to offend them personally, but that I wanted to offer civil resistance to their orders. In this way they were put at ease, and instead of harassing me they gladly availed themselves of my and my co-workers' cooperation in regulating the crowds. But it was an ocular demonstration to them of the fact that their authority was shaken. The people had for the moment lost all fear of punishment and yielded obedience to the power of love which their new friend exercised.

It should be remembered that no one knew me in Champaran. The peasants were all ignorant. Champaran, being far up north of the Ganges, and right at the foot of the Himalayas in close proximity to Nepal, was cut off from the rest of India.

No emissaries had therefore been sent there, openly or secretly, on behalf of the Congress to prepare for our arrival. Rajkumar Shukla was incapable of reaching the thousands of peasants. No political work had yet been done among them. The world outside Champaran was not known to them. And yet they received me as though we had been age-long friends. It is no exaggeration, but the literal truth, to say that in this meeting with the peasants I was face to face with God, Nonviolence, and Truth.

When I come to examine my title to this realization, I find nothing but my love for the people. And this in turn is nothing but an expression of my unshakable faith in Nonviolence.

That day in Champaran was an unforgettable event in my life and a red-letter day for the peasants and for me.

According to the law, I was to be on trial, but truly speaking, the government was to be on trial. The Commissioner only succeeded in trapping the government in the net which he had spread for me.

The trial began. The government pleader, the Magistrate, and other officials were on tenterhooks. They were at a loss to know what to do. The government pleader was pressing the Magistrate to postpone the case. But I interfered and requested the Magistrate not to postpone the case, as I wanted to plead guilty to having disobeyed the order to leave Champaran and read a brief statement as follows:

> I have entered the country with motives of rendering humanitarian and national service. I have done so in response to a pressing invitation to come and help the peasants who urge that they are not being fairly treated by the indigo planters. I could not render any help without studying the problem. I have therefore come to study it with the assistance, if possible, of the Administration and the planters. I have no other motive and cannot believe that my coming can in any way disturb public peace and cause loss of life. It is my firm belief that in the complex constitution under which we are living, the only safe and honorable course for a self-respecting man is, in the circumstances such as face me, to do what I have decided to do, that is, to submit without protest to the penalty of disobedience. I venture to make this statement not in any way in extenuation of the penalty to be awarded against me, but to show that I have disregarded the order served upon me not for want of respect for lawful authority, but in obedience to the higher law of our being, the voice of conscience.

As both the Magistrate and the government pleader had been taken by surprise, the Magistrate postponed judgment. Meanwhile I had wired full details to the Viceroy, to Patna friends, and others. Before I could appear before the court to receive the sentence, the Magistrate sent a written message that the Lieutenant Governor had ordered the case against me to be withdrawn, and the Collector wrote to me saying that I was at liberty to conduct the proposed inquiry, and that I might count on whatever help I needed from the officials. None of us was prepared for this prompt and happy issue.

The country thus had its first direct lesson in civil disobedience. The Champaran inquiry was a bold experiment with Truth and Nonviolence.

THE NATIONAL STRIKE

I happened casually to read in the papers the Rowlatt Committee's report which had just been published. Its recommendations [calling for the continuation of the removal of all civil liberties and a free press, even though World War I was ending] startled me. "Something must be done," I said to Vallabhbhai. "But what can we do in the circumstances?" he asked in reply. I answered, "If even a handful of men and women can be found to sign the pledge of resistance, and the proposed measure is passed into law in defiance of it, we ought to offer satyagraha at once. If I was not laid up like this (with an illness), I should give battle against it all alone, and expect others to follow suit. But in my present helpless condition I feel myself to be altogether unequal to the task."

As a result of this talk, it was decided to call a small meeting. The satyagraha pledge was drafted at this meeting, and signed by all present. A separate body called the Satyagraha Sabha was established.

While on the one hand the agitation against the Rowlatt Committee's report gathered volume and intensity, on the other the government grew more and more determined to give effect to its recommendations and the Rowlatt Bill was published. In these circumstances mine could only be a cry in the wilderness. I earnestly pleaded with the Viceroy. I addressed him private letters and public letters, in the course of which I clearly told him that the government's action left me no other course except to resort to satyagraha. But it was all in vain.

We daily discussed plans of the fight, but beyond the holding of public meetings, I could not then think of any other program. I felt myself at a loss to discover how to offer civil disobedience against the Rowlatt Bill if it was finally passed into law. One could disobey it only if the government gave one the opportunity for it. Failing that, could we civilly disobey other laws? And if so, where was the line to be drawn?

While these cogitations were still going on, news was received that the Rowlatt Bill had been published as an Act. That night I fell asleep while thinking over the question. Toward the small hours of the morning I woke up somewhat earlier than usual. I was still in that twilight condition between sleep and consciousness when suddenly the idea broke upon me. It was as if in a dream. Early in the morning I related the whole story to Rajagopalachari.

"The idea came to me last night in a dream that we should call upon the country to observe a general strike, a hartal. Satyagraha is a process of self-purification, and ours is a sacred fight, and it seems to me to be in the fitness of things that it should be commenced with an act of self-purification. Let all the people of India, therefore, suspend their business on that day and observe the day as a day of prayer and fasting. The Muslims may not fast for more than one day, so the duration of the fast should be for 24 hours. It is very difficult to say whether all the provinces would respond to this appeal of ours or not, but I feel fairly sure of Bombay, Madres, Bihar, and Sindh. I think we should have every reason to feel satisfied even if all these places observe the strike fittingly."

Rajagopalachari was at once taken up with my suggestion. Other friends too welcomed it when it was communicated to them later. I drafted a brief appeal. The date of the strike was fixed on April 6, 1919. The people thus had only a short notice of the strike. As the work had to be started at once, it was hardly possible to give longer notice.

But who knows how it all came about? The whole of India from one end to the other, towns as well as villages, observed a complete strike on that day. It was a most wonderful spectacle.

THE SPIRITUAL PATH
OF NONVIOLENCE AND PURITY

My uniform experience has convinced me that there is no other God than Truth. And if every page of these chapters does not proclaim to the reader that the only means for the realization of Truth is nonviolence, I shall deem all my labor in writing to have been in vain. And even though my efforts in this behalf may prove fruitless, let the reader know that the vehicle, not the great principle, is at fault. After all, however sincere my strivings after nonviolence may have been, they have still been imperfect and inadequate. The little fleeting glimpses, therefore, that I have been able to have of Truth can hardly convey an idea of the indescribable luster of Truth, a million times more intense than that of the sun we daily see with our eyes. In fact what I have caught is only the faintest glimmer of that mighty effulgence. But this much I can say with assurance, as a result of all my experiments, that a perfect vision of Truth can only follow a complete realization of Nonviolence.

To see the universal and all-pervading Spirit of Truth face to face one must be able to love the meanest of creation as oneself. And a person who aspires after that cannot afford to keep out of any field of life. That is why my devotion to Truth has drawn me into the field of politics; and I can say without the slightest hesitation, and yet in all humility, that those who say that religion has nothing to do with politics do not know what religion means.

Identification with everything that lives is impossible without self-purification. Without self-purification the observance of the law of Nonviolence must remain an empty dream. Good can never be realized by one who is not pure of heart. Self-purification therefore must mean purification in all the walks of life. And purification being highly infectious, purification of oneself necessarily leads to the purification of one's surroundings.

But the path of self-purification is hard and steep. To attain to perfect purity one has to become absolutely passion-free in thought, speech, and action; to rise above the opposing currents of love and hatred, attachment and repulsion. I know that I have not in me as yet that triple purity, in spite of constant ceaseless striving for it. That is why the world's praise fails to move me, indeed it very often stings me. To conquer the subtle passions seems to me to be far harder than the physical conquest of the world by the force of arms. Ever since my return to India, I have had experiences of the dormant passions lying hidden within me. The knowledge of them has made me feel humiliated though not defeated. The experiences and experiments have sustained me and given me great joy. But I know that I have still before me a difficult path to traverse. I must reduce myself to zero. So long as a people do not of their own free will put themselves last among their fellow creatures, there is no salvation for them. Nonviolence is the farthest limit of humility.

2

The Search for God

As Gandhi wrote in his autobiography, his one goal in life was to see God face to face. Everything he did was in search of God. And so, for the last fifty years of his life, Gandhi spent at least two hours every day in meditation and continually repeated God's name over and over in his mind throughout the day to keep him focused and centered. All his public campaigns for justice and freedom, his solidarity with the poorest of the poor, his voluntary poverty and celibacy, his civil disobedience and community life were understood as necessary components for this search for God.

Gandhi's life of prayer and scripture study led him to describe God as the God of truth, the God of nonviolence, the God of peace. As he grew to worship the God of truth and nonviolence, he deepened his own pursuit of truth and nonviolence as the mission of his life and the spiritual message he could offer the world. "We tend to become what we worship," Gandhi wrote. "We must become living embodiments of Truth and Love because God is Truth and Love." His life of prayer and nonviolence pushed him closer and closer to the God of truth and nonviolence. Though he was perceived by the British as a conniving politician and a rebel, hundreds of millions of poor Indians saw him not just as their political liberator but as their spiritual master. Gandhi called them to search for God too, and they saw in him the possibility of achieving both political independence and spiritual enlightenment.

"I am endeavoring to follow where God leads me," Gandhi wrote in 1924 to a Christian friend in South Africa. "I have no axes to grind, no worldly ambition to serve. The only purpose of life is to see God face to face, and the more I see of life and its experiences, the more I feel that everyone does not receive the light in the same way, even as, though the sun is the same, we see it differently from the equatorial regions, from the temperate zone, and from the frigid zone."

If we want to understand Gandhi and seek peace and justice for humanity as he did, we need to apply the same single-minded devotion and discipline in search of God. He would want us to give up our search for money, fame, honor, and power, and give our lives instead to the search for God. He promised that we would experience a great inner peace if we truly sought God with humble and contrite hearts, and that our lives would be used by the God of truth and nonviolence for the disarmament of the world and bear the good fruit of peace for humanity.

GOD IS TRUTH AND LOVE

To me, God is Truth and Love. God is ethics and morality. God is fearlessness. God is the source of Light and Life and yet God is above and beyond all these. God is conscience. God is even the atheism of the atheist. God transcends speech and reason. God is a personal God to those who need God's personal presence. God is embodied to those who need God's touch. God is the purest essence. God simply *is* to those who have faith. God is all things to all people. God is in us and yet above and beyond us. God is long-suffering. God is patient, but God is also terrible. With God ignorance is no excuse. And with all, God is ever forgiving for God always gives us the chance to repent. God is the greatest democrat the world knows, for God leaves us "unfettered" to make our own choice between evil and good. God is the greatest tyrant ever known, for God often dashes the cup from our lips and under the cover of free will leaves us a margin so wholly inadequate as to provide only mirth for himself.

—Vol. 26, March 5, 1925

THE UNSEEN POWER

There is an indefinable mysterious Power that pervades everything. I feel it, though I do not see it. It is this unseen Power which makes itself felt and yet defies all proof, because it is so unlike all that I perceive through my senses. It transcends the senses. But it is possible to reason out the existence of God to a limited extent.

But God is no God who merely satisfies the intellect, if God ever does. God to be God must rule the heart and transform it. God must express himself in even the smallest act of his votary. This can only be done through a definite realization more real than the five senses can ever produce. Sense perceptions can be, and often are, false and deceptive, however real they may appear to us. Where there is realization outside the sense it is infallible. It is proved not by extraneous evidence but in the transformed conduct and character of those who have felt the real presence of God within. Such testimony is to be found in the experiences of an unbroken line of prophets and sages in all countries and climates. To reject this evidence is to deny oneself.

—Vol. 38, October 11, 1928

•

I do dimly perceive that while everything around me is ever changing, ever dying, there is underlying all that change a Living Power that is changeless, that holds all together, that creates, dissolves, and re-creates. That informing Power or Spirit is God. And since nothing else I see merely through the senses can or will persist, God alone is.

And is this Power benevolent or malevolent? I see it as purely benevolent. For I can see that in the midst of death, life persists. In the midst of untruth, truth persists. In the midst of darkness,

light persists. Hence I gather that God is Life, Truth, Light. God
is love.

I know, too, that I shall never know God if I do not wrestle
with and against evil even at the cost of life itself. I am for-
tified in the belief by my own humble and limited experience.
The purer I try to become, the nearer to God I feel myself to be.
How much more should I be near to God when my faith is not a
mere apology, as it is today, but has become as immovable as the
Himalayas and as white and bright as the snows on their peaks?

—Vol. 29, October 11, 1925

TRUTH IS GOD

In my early youth, I was taught to repeat what in Hindu scriptures are known as the one thousand names of God. But these
one thousand names of God were by no means exhaustive. We
believe, and I think it is the truth, that God has as many names
as there are creatures. Therefore, we also say that God is nameless, and since God has many forms, we consider God formless,
and since God speaks through many tongues, we consider God
to be speechless and so on. And so, when I came to study Islam,
I found Islam too had many names of God.

I would say with those who say "God is Love," God is Love.
But deep down in me, I used to say that though God may be
Love, God is Truth above all. If it is possible for the human
tongue to give the fullest description of God, I have come to
the conclusion that God is Truth. Two years ago, I went a step
further and said that Truth is God. You will see the fine distinction between the two statements, "God is Truth," and "Truth is
God." I came to that conclusion after a continuous and relentless search after truth which began fifty years ago. I then found
that the nearest approach to truth was through love. But I also
found that love has many meanings in the English language, and
that human love in the sense of passion could become a degrading thing. I found too that love in the sense of nonviolence had
only a limited number of votaries in the world. But I never found

a double meaning in connection with truth, and even atheists had not demurred to the necessity of the power of truth. But in their passion for discovering truth, atheists have not hesitated to deny the very existence of God, from their own point of view rightly. It was because of this reasoning that I saw that rather than say that God is Truth, I should say that Truth is God.

Add to this the great difficulty that millions have taken the name of God and in God's name committed nameless atrocities. Not that the scientists very often do not commit atrocities in the name of Truth. Then there is another thing in Hindu philosophy, namely, God alone is and nothing else exists, and the same truth you see emphasized and exemplified in Islam. And there you find it clearly stated that God alone is, and nothing else exists. In fact, the Sanskrit word for truth is a word which literally means "that which exists," *sat*. For these and many other reasons, I have come to the conclusion that the definition — Truth is God — gives me the greatest satisfaction. And when you want to find Truth as God, the only inevitable means is love, that is, nonviolence, and since I believe that ultimately the means and ends are convertible terms, I should not hesitate to say that God is Love.

— *All Men Are Brothers,* 63–64

THE REQUIREMENT OF A LIVING FAITH

This belief in God has to be based on faith which transcends reason. Indeed, even the so-called realization has at bottom an element of faith without which it cannot be sustained. In the very nature of things it must be so. Who can transgress the limitations of one's being? I hold that complete realization is impossible in this embodied life. Nor is it necessary. A living immovable faith is all that is required for reaching the full spiritual height attainable by human beings. God is not outside this earthly case of ours. Therefore, exterior proof is not of much avail, if any at all. We must ever fail to perceive God through the senses, because God is beyond them. We can feel God, if we will but withdraw ourselves from the senses. The divine music is incessantly going on within ourselves, but the loud senses drown the delicate music, which is unlike and infinitely superior to anything we can perceive or hear with our senses.   —Vol. 63, June 13, 1936

•

If we exist, if our parents and their parents have existed, then it is proper to believe in the Parent of the whole creation. If God is not, we are nowhere. God is one yet many; God is smaller than an atom and bigger than the Himalayas. God is contained even in a drop of the ocean, and yet not even the seven seas can compass God. Reason is powerless to know God. God is beyond the reach or grasp of reason. But I need not labor the point. Faith is essential in this matter. My logic can make and unmake innumerable hypotheses. An atheist might floor me in a debate. But my faith runs so very much faster than my reason that I can challenge the whole world and say, "God is, was, and ever shall be."

But those who want to deny God's existence are at liberty to do so. God is merciful and compassionate. God is not an earthly king needing an army to make us accept God's sway. God allows us freedom, and yet God's compassion commands obedience to God's will. But if any one of us disdain to bow to God's will, God says, "So be it. My sun will shine no less for you, my clouds will rain no less for you. I need not force you to accept my sway." Of such a God let the ignorant dispute the existence. I am one of the millions who believe in God and am never tired of bowing to God and singing God's glory.   —Vol. 29, January 21, 1926

•

God is the hardest taskmaster I have known on earth, and God tries you through and through. And when you find your faith is failing or your body is failing you, and you are sinking, God comes to your assistance somehow or other, and proves to you that you must not lose your faith and that God is always at your beck and call, but on God's terms, not on your terms.

                                        —My Religion, 45

FINDING GOD
THROUGH SERVING HUMANITY

I am endeavoring to see God through service of humanity, for I know that God is neither in heaven, nor down below, but in everyone.　　　　　　　　　　　—Vol. 33, August 4, 1927

Humanity's ultimate aim is the realization of God and all our activities — political, social, and religious — have to be guided by the ultimate aim of the vision of God. The immediate service of all human beings becomes a necessary part of the endeavor simply because the only way to find God is to see God in God's creation and be one with it. This can only be done by service of all. And this cannot be done except through one's country. I am a part and parcel of the whole, and I cannot find God apart from the rest of the humanity. My compatriots are my nearest neighbors. They have become so helpless, so resourceless, so inert that I must concentrate on serving them. If I could persuade myself that I should find God in a Himalayan cave I would proceed there immediately. But I know that I cannot find God apart from humanity.　　　　　　　　—Vol. 63, August 29, 1936

I could not be leading a religious life unless I identified myself with the whole of humanity, and that I could not do unless I took part in politics. The whole gamut of humanity's activities constitutes an indivisible whole. You cannot divide social, economic, political, and purely religious work into watertight compartments. I do not know any religion apart from human activity. It provides a moral basis to all other activities which they would otherwise lack, reducing life to a maze of "sound and fury signifying nothing."　　　　　　　　—Vol. 62, December 24, 1935

•

I am a humble seeker after truth. I am impatient to realize myself, to attain salvation in this very existence. My national service is part of my training for freeing my soul from the bondage of flesh. Thus, my service may be regarded as purely selfish. I have no desire for a perishable kingdom of earth. I am striving for the Kingdom of Heaven, which is salvation. To attain my end, it is not necessary for me to seek the shelter of a cave. I carry one about me, if I would but know it. For me, the road to salvation lies through incessant toil in the service of my country and so all humanity. I want to identify myself with everything that lives. In the language of the Gita, I want to live at peace with both friend and foe. Though a Muslim or a Christian or a Hindu may despise me and hate me, I want to love him and serve him even as I would love my wife or son though they hate me. So my patriotism is for me a stage in my journey to the land of eternal freedom and peace. Thus it will be seen that for me there are no politics devoid of religion. They subserve religion. Politics bereft of religion are a death-trap because they kill the soul.

—Vol. 23, April 3, 1924

For me, politics bereft of religion are absolute dirt ever to be shunned. Politics concern nations and that which concerns the welfare of nations must be one of the concerns of a person who is religiously inclined, in other words, a seeker after God and Truth. For me, God and Truth are convertible terms, and if anyone told me that God was a God of untruth or a God of torture, I would decline to worship him. Therefore, in politics also we have to establish the Kingdom of Heaven.   —Vol. 28, June 18, 1925

I have had my share of disappointments, uttermost darkness, de-spair, caution, subtlest assault of pride, but I am able to say that my faith — and I know that it is still little enough, by no means as great as I want it to be — has ultimately conquered every one of these difficulties up to now. If we have faith in us, if we have a prayerful heart, we may not tempt God or make terms with God. We must reduce ourselves to ciphers. A precious Sanskrit verse says that people of devotion reduce themselves to zero. Not until we have reduced ourselves to nothingness can we conquer the evil in us. God demands nothing less than complete self-surrender as the price for the only real freedom that is worth having. And we thus lose ourselves, we immediately find ourselves in the service of all that lives. It becomes our delight and our recreation. We are new persons, never weary of spending ourselves in the service of God's creation. —Vol. 38, December 20, 1928

GOD IS WITHIN ALL OF US

I believe that we can all become messengers of God, if we cease to fear others and seek only God's Truth. I do believe I am seeking only God's Truth and have lost all fear of people. I do feel that God is with the movement of noncooperation. I have no special revelation of God's will. My firm belief is that God reveals himself daily to every human being, but we shut our ears to that "still small voice." We shut our eyes to the "pillar of fire" in front of us. —Vol. 20, May 25, 1921

If I did not feel the presence of God within me, since I see so much of misery and disappointment every day, I would be a raving maniac. —Vol. 28, August 6, 1925

God is present in all of us. For my part, every moment I experience the truth that though many, we are all one. God does not reveal himself in the same form in all of us, or rather the heart of all of us not being alike, we do not see God in the same form — just as in mirrors of different colors and shapes a thing is reflected in different colors and shapes.

From this it follows that the sin of one is the sin of all. And hence it is not up to us to destroy the evildoer. We should, on the contrary, suffer for him. From this thought was born the idea of satyagraha and of civil disobedience to unjust law. Criminal, violent, or uncivil disobedience is a sin and ought to be abjured. Nonviolent disobedience can be a holy duty.
—Vol. 43, March 16, 1930

•

I must go with God as my only guide. God is a jealous Lord. God will allow no one to share God's authority. One has, therefore, to

appear before God in all one's weakness, empty-handed and in a
spirit of full surrender, and then God enables you to stand before
a whole world and protects you from all harm.

—Vol. 47, September 3, 1931

•

The purpose of life is undoubtedly to know oneself. We cannot
do it unless we learn to identify ourselves with all that lives. The
sum total of that life is God. Hence the necessity of realizing God
living within every one of us. The instrument of this knowledge
is boundless selfless service.   —Vol. 50, June 21, 1932

RESPECT ALL RELIGIONS

I believe in the fundamental truth of all great religions of the
world. I believe that they are all God-given, and I believe that
they were necessary for the people to whom these religions were
revealed. And I believe that, if only we could all of us read the
scriptures of different faiths from the standpoint of the followers
of those faiths, we should find that they were at bottom all one
and were all helpful to one another.

—Vol. 57, February 16, 1934

I am a believer in the truth of all the great religions of the world.
There will be no lasting peace on earth unless we learn not merely
to tolerate but even to respect the other faiths as our own. A
reverent study of the sayings of different teachers of humanity is
a step in the direction of such mutual respect.

—*Selected Works,* Vol. 6, 268

CHRIST'S GOSPEL OF LOVE AND PEACE

Christ came into this world to preach and spread the gospel of
love and peace, but what his followers have brought about is

tyranny and misery. Christians who were taught the maxim of "Love thy neighbor as thyself," are divided among themselves.

—Vol. 63, August 3, 1947

Today I rebel against orthodox Christianity, as I am convinced that it has distorted the message of Jesus. He was an Asiatic whose message was delivered through many media, and when it had the backing of a Roman emperor it became an imperialist faith as it remains to this day.   —Vol. 62, May 30, 1936

Jesus was the most active resister known perhaps to history. His was nonviolence par excellence.   —Vol. 84, June 26, 1946

Jesus expressed, as no other could, the spirit and will of God. It is in this sense that I see him and recognize him as the Son of God. And because the life of Jesus has the significance and the transcendency to which I have alluded, I believe that he belongs not solely to Christianity, but to the entire world, to all races and people.   —Vol. 74, October 1941

What would not I have given to be able to bow my head before the living image at the Vatican of Christ Crucified? It was with a wrench that I could tear myself away from the scene of living tragedy. I saw there at once that nations like individuals could only be made through the agony of the Cross and in no other way. Joy comes not out of infliction of pain on others but out of pain voluntarily borne by oneself.

I consider Western Christianity in its practical working a negation of Christ's Christianity. I cannot conceive Jesus, if he was living in the flesh in our midst, approving of modern Christian organizations, public worship, or modern ministry. If Christians will simply cling to the Sermon on the Mount, which was delivered not merely to the peaceful disciples but a groaning world, they would not go wrong, and they would find that no religion is false, and that if they act according to their lights and in the fear of God, they would not need to worry about organizations, forms of worship, and ministry. The Pharisees had all that, but Jesus would have none of it, for they were using their office as a cloak for hypocrisy and worse. Cooperation with the forces of Good and noncooperation with the forces of evil are the two things we need for a good and pure life, whether it is called Hindu, Muslim, or Christian.   —Vol. 21, 1921

Christ never answered a question in a simple and literal manner. He always gave in his replies more than was expected, something deeper, some general principle. It was so in this case [when he said, "Render to Caesar the things that are Caesar's, and to God the things that are God's"]. Here he does not mean at all whether you must or must not pay taxes. He means something far more than this. When he says "Render to Caesar the things which are Caesar's," he is stating a law. It means, "Give back to Caesar what is his — I will have nothing to do with it." In this incident, Christ enunciated the great law, which he exemplified all his life, of refusing to cooperate with evil. When Satan said to him, "Bow and worship me," that is, cooperate with me, then Christ said, "Get behind me, Satan." When the crowds around him wanted to take him by force and make him a military king, he refused to cooperate with them as their method was evil. They wanted him to rely on military force. Christ's attitude against the authorities was defiant. When Pilate asked him if he were a king, he answered, "You say it." Is not that treating authority with defiance? He called Herod "that fox." Was that cooperation with authorities? And before Herod he would not answer a word. In short, Christ refused to cooperate with Herod, and so I refuse to cooperate with the British government.
                    —From an interview in jail, Vol. 23, March 18, 1922

COMPASSION AND SOLIDARITY
WITH THE POOR

Religion without compassion is a fraud. Compassion is at the very root of religion, and one who forsakes it, forsakes God. One who forsakes the poor forsakes everything. If we do not look after the poor and the untouchables, we are sure to perish.

—Vol. 25, January 25, 1925

God can be served in one way alone. To serve the poor is to serve God.

What is the aim of life? It is to know the self. This realization of the self, or self-knowledge, is not possible until one has achieved unity with all living beings, until one has become one with God. To accomplish such a unity implies deliberate sharing of the suffering of others and the eradication of such suffering.

—Vol. 28, October 25, 1925

•

My experience tells me that the Kingdom of God is within us, and that we can realize it not by saying, "Lord, Lord," but by doing God's will and God's work. If therefore we wait for the Kingdom to come as something coming from outside, we shall be sadly mistaken. Do you know that there are thousands of villages where people are starving and which are on the brink of ruin? If we would listen to the voice of God, I assure you we would hear God say that we are taking God's name in vain if we do not think of the poor and help them. If you cannot render the help that they need, it is no use talking of service of God and service of the poor. Try to identify yourselves with the poor by actually helping them.

—Vol. 33, March 31, 1927

JOY IN THE SEARCH FOR GOD

There is only one joy for me and that is to get a glimpse of God. This will be possible when I become one with the poor. I can be one with the whole world if I can merge myself in the poor people of a poor country.   —Vol. 63, November 8, 1936

•

Lovers of Truth feel undiminished joy till the end of life. They never regard themselves as too old to keep on striving for a vision of the God of Truth. Those who undertake every activity in order to see God, also called Truth, who see Truth in everything that exists, will not find old age an obstacle to the quest. So far as that quest is concerned, seekers regard themselves as immortal and forever young.   —Vol. 49, April 14, 1932

•

I have been a willing slave to this most exacting Master for more than half a century. God's voice has been increasingly audible as years have rolled by. God has never forsaken me even in my darkest hour. God has saved me often against myself and left me not a vestige of independence. The greater the surrender to God, the greater has been my joy.   —*My Religion,* 45

3

The Pursuit of Truth

In his search for God, Gandhi concluded that God is Truth, and then, that Truth is God. With this spiritual understanding, Gandhi ruthlessly pursued the truth in every facet of his life and in the world. But he immediately realized that the only way to truth was through nonviolence. He could never hurt or kill another in his insistence on the truth, much less wage war to defend what he thought was the truth.

The genius of Gandhi was not only his spiritual search for God as Truth, but his social and political application of that spiritual search for truth. In 1908, while organizing the movement for the truth of social justice and racial equality in South Africa, he coined the word "satyagraha" to describe this mass pursuit of truth by entire peoples and nations. Gandhi defined satyagraha as "holding to Truth," "clinging to Truth" "pursuing Truth," or "truth-force," as well as "steadfast, nonviolent direct action for truth" and "nonviolent civil disobedience."

For the rest of his life, Gandhi pursued Truth, whether in South Africa or India, in terms of the practice of Satyagraha. He tried to "experiment with truth" as a scientist labors in the laboratory, only his laboratory grew to include not just his heart and household but an entire nation and the world. He inspired others to give their freedom and their lives in the pursuit of the truth of justice, freedom, and peace. Gandhi said that satyagraha or the organized, steadfast pursuit of truth could be used by any group as a way to liberation and justice. He was con-

vinced it would always work, and he proved this in countless episodes throughout his life. He also insisted that this non-violent pursuit of truth would require voluntary suffering and sacrifice. In that spirit, he spent nearly six years of his life in prison and was eventually martyred.

"I am devoted to none but Truth and I owe no discipline to anybody but Truth," Gandhi wrote. "I am but a seeker after Truth. I claim to have found a way to it. I claim to be making a ceaseless effort to find it. But I admit that I have not found it. To find Truth completely is to realize oneself and one's destiny, to become perfect." "Realizing Truth," Gandhi wrote shortly before his assassination, "means realizing that all human beings are one."

DEVOTION TO TRUTH

The word *Satya* (Truth) is derived from *Sat*, which means "being." Nothing is or exists in reality except Truth. That is why *Sat* or Truth is perhaps the most important name of God. In fact it is more correct to say that Truth is God, than to say that God is Truth.

Devotion to this Truth is the sole justification for our existence. All our activities should be centered in Truth. Truth should be the very breath of our life. When once this state in the pilgrim's progress is reached, all other rules of correct living will come without effort, and obedience to them will be instinctive. But without Truth it would be impossible to observe any principles or rules in life.

Generally speaking, observation of the law of Truth is understood merely to mean that we must speak the truth. But we in the Ashram should understand the word *Satya* or Truth in a much wider sense. There should be Truth in thought, Truth in speech, and Truth in action.

But Truth is the right designation of God. Hence there is nothing wrong in everyone following Truth according to their own lights. Indeed, it is their duty to do so. Then if there is a mistake on the part of anyone so following Truth, it will be automatically set right. For the quest of Truth involves *tapas* — self-suffering, sometimes even death. There can be no place in it for even a trace of self-interest. In such selfless search for Truth nobody can lose their bearings for long. When they take to the wrong path and stumble, they are redirected to the right path. Therefore the pursuit of Truth is true *bhakti* (devotion). It is the path that leads to God.

How beautiful it would be, if all of us, young and old, men and women, devoted ourselves wholly to Truth in all that we might do in our waking hours, whether working, eating, drinking or playing, till dissolution of the body makes us one with Truth? God as Truth has been for me a treasure beyond price. May God be so to every one of us.

—Vol. 44, July 22, 1930; revised in 1945

•

Truth is the first thing to be sought for, and Beauty and Goodness will then be added to you. This is what Christ really taught in the Sermon on the Mount. Jesus was, to my mind, a supreme artist because he saw and expressed Truth; and so was Muhammad, the Koran being the most perfect composition in all Arabic literature. It is because both of them strove first for Truth that the grace of expression naturally came in and yet neither Jesus nor Muhammad wrote on art. That is the Truth and Beauty I crave for, live for, and would die for.   —Vol. 24, November 20, 1924

•

To tread the path of truth implies an active life in the world. In the absence of such activity, there is no occasion for either pursuing or swerving from truth. The Gita has made it clear that a person cannot remain inactive even for a single moment. The difference between one who is a devotee of God and another who is not is that the former is active in the service of others, never gives up truth in the midst of activity, and gradually overcomes his likes and dislikes, while the other is active for selfish reasons, and has no scruples whatever as regards the means he employs in order to achieve his selfish ends. This world is not something evil in itself, for only an active life in the world can help us to attain the goal of God-realization. This activity must be directed to the good of others. Selfish activity is fit only to be condemned and should be given up.   —Vol. 50, July 24, 1932

THE METHOD OF SATYAGRAHA

For the past thirty years, I have been preaching and practicing Satyagraha. Satyagraha differs from passive resistance as the North Pole from the South. The latter has been conceived as a weapon of the weak and does not exclude the use of physical force or violence for the purpose of gaining one's end, whereas the former has been conceived as a weapon of the strongest and excludes the use of violence in any shape or form.

The term "Satyagraha" was coined by me in South Africa to express the force that the Indians there used for a full eight years, and it was coined in order to distinguish it from the movement then going on in the United Kingdom and South Africa under the name of "Passive Resistance."

Its root meaning is "holding on to truth," hence "Truth-force." I have also called it "Love-force" or "Soul-force." In the application of satyagraha, I discovered in the earliest stages that pursuit of truth did not admit of violence being inflicted on one's opponent but that he must be weaned from error by patience and sympathy. For what appears to be truth to the one may appear to be error to the other. And patience means self-suffering. So the doctrine came to mean vindication of Truth not by infliction of suffering on the opponent but on one's self.

But on the political field the struggle on behalf of the people mostly consists in opposing error in the shape of unjust laws. When you have failed to bring the error home to the lawgiver by way of petitions and the like, the only remedy open to you, if you do not wish to submit to error, is to compel the lawgiver by physical force to yield to you or by suffering in your own person by inviting the penalty for the breach of the law. Hence satyagraha largely appears to the public as civil disobedience or civil resistance. It is civil in the sense that it is not criminal.

The lawbreaker breaks the law surreptitiously and tries to avoid the penalty, but not so the civil resisters. They ever obey the laws of the state to which they belong, not out of fear of the sanctions but because they consider them to be good for the welfare of society. But there come occasions, generally rare, when they consider certain laws to be so unjust as to render obedience to them a dishonor. They then openly and civilly break them and quietly suffer the penalty for their breach. And in order to register their protest against the action of the lawgivers, it is open to them to withdraw their cooperation from the state by disobeying such other laws whose breach does not involve moral turpitude.

In my opinion the beauty and efficacy of satyagraha are so great and the doctrine so simple that it can be preached even to children. It was preached by me to thousands of men, women, and children commonly called indentured Indians with excellent results.   —*Selected Works,* Vol. 6, January 14, 1920, 178–80

•

Satyagraha is literally holding on to Truth, and it means, therefore, Truth-force. Truth is soul or spirit. It is, therefore, known as Soul-force. It excludes the use of violence because humanity is not capable of knowing the absolute truth and, therefore, not competent to punish. Noncooperation and civil disobedience are branches of satyagraha, which includes all nonviolent resistance for the vindication of truth.   —Vol. 19, March 23, 1921

Satyagraha is a relentless search for truth and a determination to reach truth.
        —*Selected Works,* Vol. 6, March 19, 1925, 185

For the exercise of the purest Truth-force, prolonged training of the individual soul is an absolute necessity, so that a perfect satyagrahi has to be almost, if not entirely, a perfect person. We cannot all suddenly become such people, but if my proposition is correct, the greater the spirit of satyagraha in us, the better people will we become. Its use, therefore, is, I think indisputable, and it is a force, which, if it became universal, would revolutionize social ideals and do away with despotisms and the ever grow-ing militarism under which the nations of the West are groaning and are being almost crushed to death, and which fairly promises to overwhelm even the nations of the East. If the past struggle has produced even a few Indians who would dedicate themselves to the task of becoming satyagrahis as nearly perfect as possible, they would not only have served themselves in the truest sense of the term, they would also have served humanity at large. Thus viewed, satyagraha is the noblest and best education. It should be an essential of real education that a child should learn that in the struggle of life, one can easily conquer hate by love, untruth by truth, violence by self-suffering.

— *Selected Works,* Vol. 6, November 3, 1927, 184–85

Satyagraha is gentle, it never wounds. It must not be the result of anger or malice. It is never fussy, never impatient, never vocifer-ous. It is the direct opposite of compulsion. It was conceived as a complete substitute for violence.

— *Selected Works,* Vol. 6, April 15, 1938, 186

•

It is a divine law that the one who serves Truth — God — will never suffer defeat. Sometimes people of truth appear to have failed, but that is no more than a fleeting appearance. In real-ity they are not defeated. When the result is not as we wanted it to be, we tend to think we have failed. But that which appears a defeat to us is often but victory itself. There are thousands of such instances in history. If with some measure of truth on our side, we strive for a certain result and fail, the blame does not lie with truth but with us. If a particular result does not serve our good, God will not grant it, however much we may desire it. That is why we quote a verse from the Gita, which says that we must fight on, with an equal mind, through happiness and unhappiness, gain and loss. If we do so, we shall incur no sin. This is a time-honored solution. With that key, we shall be able to open the most unyielding of locks. The one who fights in this manner will fight only in the name of God. That person will give no thought to success or failure. That person is pledged only to the great task of serving Truth, doing one's duty in the name of God. The outcome itself is in the hands of God Almighty.

—Vol. 8, February 8, 1908

•

Satyagraha is both easy and difficult. I think it should be easy by now for everyone to see that every grievance can be remedied if we make it a point to follow nothing but the truth. It is difficult to observe truth, to suffer in order to put an end to suffering. And yet, the more I think about it, the more I see that there is no other way than that of satyagraha for us to fight our ills and those of others. I even feel that the world has no other really effective remedy to offer. Be that as it may, we at least have realized that it is better to win through satyagraha. Let us constantly remind ourselves that all the nations that have risen high have braved extreme suffering. If we want to rise high, we must adopt the same means.   —Vol. 9, October 17, 1908

THE QUALITIES OF A SATYAGRAHI

Satyagrahis [those who cling to the truth] bear no ill will, do not lay down their life in anger, but refuse rather to submit to their "enemy" or oppressor because the satyagrahis have the strength within to suffer. Satyagrahis should, therefore, have a courageous spirit and a forgiving and compassionate nature. Satyagraha is the way of nonviolence. It is therefore justified; indeed it is the right course, at all times and in all places. The power of arms is violence and condemned as such in all religions. Even those who advocate the use of arms put various limits on it. There are no limits on satyagraha, or rather, none except those placed by the satyagrahi's capacity for voluntary suffering.

—Vol. 13, September 2, 1917

•

The Indians of South Africa believed that Truth was their object, that Truth ever triumphs, and with this definiteness of purpose, they persistently held on to Truth. They put up with all the suffering that this persistence implied. With the conviction that Truth is not to be renounced even unto death, they shed the fear of death. In the cause of Truth, the prison was a palace to them and its doors the gateway to freedom.

Satyagraha is not physical force. A satyagrahi does not inflict pain on the adversary. A satyagrahi does not seek the adversary's destruction. A satyagrahi never resorts to weapons. In the use of satyagraha, there is no ill will whatsoever. Satyagraha is pure soul-force. Truth is the very substance of the soul. That is why this force is called Satyagraha.   — Vol. 13, September 2, 1917

•

Satyagrahis do not fear for their body. Satyagrahis do not give up what they think is Truth. The word "defeat" is not to be found in their dictionary. Satyagrahis do not wish for the destruction of their antagonists. Satyagrahis do not vent anger on them, but have only compassion for them. Satyagrahis do not wait for others, but throw themselves into the fray, relying entirely on their own resources. They trust that when the time comes, others will do likewise. Their practice is their precept. Like air, satyagraha is all-pervading. It is infectious, which means that all people — big and small, men and women — can become satyagrahis. No one is kept out from the army of satyagrahis. Satyagrahis cannot perpetrate tyranny on anyone. They are not subdued through application of physical force. They do not strike at anyone. Satyagraha means that what we want is truth, that we deserve it, and that we will work for it even unto death.

— Vol. 13, September 5, 1917

•

Satyagrahis must never forget the distinction between evil and the evildoer. They must not harbor ill will or bitterness against the evildoer. They may not even employ needlessly offensive language against evildoing persons, however unrelieved their evil might be. For it should be an article of faith with every satya-grahi that there is none so fallen in this world that cannot be converted by love. Satyagrahis will always try to overcome evil by good, anger by love, untruth by truth, violence by nonviolence. There is no other way of purging the world of evil. Therefore those who claim to be satyagrahis always try by close and prayer-ful self-introspection and self-analysis to find out whether they are themselves completely free from the taint of anger, ill will, and such other human infirmities, whether they are not them-selves capable of these very evils against which they are out to lead a crusade. In self-purification and penance lies half the vic-tory of a satyagrahi. A satyagrahi has faith that the silent and undemonstrative action of truth and love produces far more per-manent and abiding results than speeches or such other showy performances.   —Vol. 41, August 8, 1929

•

In the dictionary of satyagraha there is no enemy. Satyagrahis love the so-called "enemy" as their friend.
                    —Vol. 70, September 11, 1939

THE WILLINGNESS
TO SUFFER FOR TRUTH

Satyagraha means fighting injustice by voluntarily submitting oneself to suffering.   —Vol. 14, January 24, 1918

Satyagraha is not a way of fighting to which one can resort unless one has a real grievance. It requires more heroism than does fight-ing a battle. Soldiers have weapons in their hands; their aim is to strike the enemy. Satyagrahis, on the contrary, fight by suffering themselves. Surely, this is not for the weak and the diffident. Such a one would not be equal to the suffering. The greater the suffer-ing that satyagrahis go through, the purer they become. As gold is tested in fire, so also do the satyagrahis have to go through a fiery ordeal. Their only weapon is uncompromising insistence on

truth. True satyagrahis fear nothing and hold fast to truth as they
fight.   —Vol. 14, April 23, 1918

Victory attained by violence is tantamount to a defeat, for it is
momentary. Then there is increase of ill will between both parties
and each prepares to give battle to the other. There is no such
untoward end to satyagraha. Satyagrahis by reason of suffering
for their principles draw toward themselves universal sympathy
and even melt the heart of the so-called enemy.
                                            —Vol. 15, May 3, 1919

Satyagraha tells the youth of India, self-suffering is the only sure
road to salvation — economic, political, and spiritual.
                                         —Vol. 16, August 20, 1919

•

As I proceed in my quest for Truth, it grows upon me that Truth
comprehends everything. I often feel that nonviolence is in Truth,
not vice versa. What is perceived by a pure heart at a particular moment is Truth to it for that moment. By clinging to it, one
can attain pure Truth. We have to live a life of nonviolence in
the midst of a world of violence, and we can do so only if we
cling to Truth. That is why I can derive nonviolence from truth.
Out of Truth emerge love and tenderness. A votary of Truth, one
who would scrupulously cling to Truth, must be utterly humble.
His humility should increase with his observance of Truth. I see
the truth of this every moment of my life. Wife, children, friends,
possessions — all should be held subject to Truth. We can be
satyagrahis only if we are ready to sacrifice each one of these in
our search for Truth.
                          —Letter from jail, Vol. 23, March 16, 1922

The idea behind the imprisonment of satyagrahis is that they expect relief through humble submission to suffering. They believe
that meek suffering for a just cause has a virtue all its own and
infinitely greater than the virtue of the sword.
                                            —Vol. 24, June 5, 1924

Suffering injury in one's own person is of the essence of non-violence and is the chosen substitute for violence to others. It is not because I value life low that I countenance with joy thousands voluntarily losing their lives in Satyagraha, but because I know that it results, in the long run, in the least loss of life and, what is more, it ennobles those who lose their lives and morally enriches the world for their sacrifice.

—Vol. 28, October 8, 1925

•

To lay down our life, even alone, for what we consider to be right, is the very core of satyagraha. More no one can do. If we are armed with a sword, we might lop off a few heads, but ultimately we must surrender to superior force or else die fighting. The sword of the satyagrahi is love and the unshakable firmness that comes from it. Satyagrahis will regard as brothers and sisters the hundreds of rioters that confront them, and instead of trying to kill them, they will choose to die at their hands and thereby live.   —Vol. 83, March 6, 1946

4

The Practice of Nonviolence

In his search for God and truth, Mohandas Gandhi concluded that he could never hurt or kill anyone, much less remain passive in the face of injustice, imperialism, and war. Instead, Gandhi dedicated himself to the practice and promotion of nonviolence. He concluded that nonviolence is not only the most powerful force there is; it is the spiritual practice most neglected and most needed throughout the world.

"Nonviolence means avoiding injury to anything on earth, in thought, word, or deed," Gandhi told an interviewer in 1935. But for Gandhi, nonviolence meant not just refraining from physical violence interpersonally and nationally, but refraining from the inner violence of the heart as well. It meant the practice of active love toward one's oppressors and enemies in the pursuit of justice, truth, and peace. "Nonviolence cannot be preached," he insisted. "It has to be practiced." For fifty years, Gandhi sought to practice nonviolence at every level in life, in his own heart, among his family and friends, and publicly in his struggle for equality in South Africa and freedom for India. It was the means by which he sought the ends of truth; in fact, he later concluded that the ends were in the means, or perhaps they were even the same. In other words, the practice of nonviolence is not just the way to peace; it is the way to God.

Gandhi's nonviolence was a religious duty. It stood at the center of his spirituality, all his spiritual teachings, and his daily spiritual practice. Gandhi concluded that God is nonviolent, and that God's reign is the reign of nonviolence. "Nonviolence assumes entire reliance upon God," Gandhi taught. "When the practice of nonviolence becomes universal, God will reign on earth as God reigns in heaven." After years of studying the various religions, Gandhi concluded too that nonviolence is at the heart of every religion. It is the common ground of all the world's religions, the hidden ground of peace and love underlying every religion.

"I am but a humble explorer of the science of nonviolence," Gandhi said. Indeed, Gandhi is the greatest apostle of nonviolence in modern history. He applied the love ethic of the New Testament and the Bhagavad Gita on a massive social and political level, and so explored the possibilities of peace and justice as never before. His political and spiritual teachings have transformed the modern world and still hold the key to social change.

Gandhi thought that the force of nonviolence was more powerful than all nuclear weapons combined and that if we all practiced perfect active nonviolence, we could unleash a spiritual explosion more powerful than the atomic bombing of Hiroshima. "I am certain that if we want to bring about peace in the world," Gandhi told a group of visitors a few months before his death, "there is no other way except that of nonviolence."

"Nonviolence is the greatest and most active force in the world," Gandhi wrote. "One person who can express nonviolence in life exercises a force superior to all the forces of brutality. My optimism rests on my belief in the infinite possibilities of the individual to develop nonviolence. The more you develop it in your own being, the more infectious it becomes till it overwhelms your surroundings and by and by might oversweep the world."

NONVIOLENCE IS
THE MOST ACTIVE FORCE
IN THE WORLD

Nonviolence is the greatest force at the disposal of humanity. It is mightier than the mightiest weapon of destruction devised by the ingenuity of humanity. Destruction is not the law of humans. Humans live freely by their readiness to die, if need be, at the hands of a brother, never by killing another. Every murder or injury no matter for what cause, committed or inflicted on another, is a crime against humanity.   —Vol. 61, July 20, 1931

Nonviolence is not passivity in any shape or form. Nonviolence, as I understand it, is the most active force in the world. Nonviolence is the supreme law. During my half a century of experience, I have not yet come across a situation when I had to say that I was helpless, that I had no remedy in terms of nonviolence.
                              —*Nonviolence in Peace and War,*
                              Vol. 1, December 24, 1935

The first condition of nonviolence is justice all around in every department of life.   —*All Men Are Brothers,* 77

Just as one must learn the art of killing in the training for violence, so one must learn the art of dying in the training for nonviolence. Violence does not mean emancipation from fear, but discovering the means of combating the cause of fear. Nonviolence on the other hand has no cause for fear. The votary of nonviolence has to cultivate the capacity for sacrifice of the highest type in order to be free from fear. The votary of nonviolence has only one fear, that is of God.
                              —*All Men Are Brothers,* 77–78

Literally, nonviolence means "nonkilling." But to me, it has a world of meaning and takes me into realms much higher, infinitely higher, than the realm to which I would go if I merely understood nonviolence as nonkilling. Nonviolence really means that you may not offend anybody. You may not harbor an uncharitable thought even in connection with those who may consider themselves to be your enemy. Pray notice the guarded nature of this thought. I do not say "whom you consider your enemy," but "who may consider themselves your enemy." For those who follow the doctrine of nonviolence, there is no room for an enemy; they deny the existence of an enemy. But there are people who consider themselves to be their enemies, and they cannot help it. So it is held that we may not harbor an evil thought even in connection with such persons. If we return blow for blow, we depart from the doctrine of nonviolence. But I go further. If we resent a friend's action or the so-called enemy's action, we still fall short of this doctrine. But when I say we should not resent, I do not say that we should acquiesce. By resenting I mean wishing that some harm should be done to the enemy, or that the enemy should be put out of the way, not even by any action of ours, but by the action of somebody else, or say by divine agency. If we harbor even this thought, we commit a breach of nonviolence. Those who join the ashram have literally to accept that meaning. That does not mean that we practice this doctrine in its entirety. Far from it. It is an ideal which we have to reach, and it is an ideal to be reached even at this very moment if we were capable of doing so. But it is not a proposition in geometry to be learned by heart; it is not even like solving difficult problems in higher mathematics; it is infinitely more difficult than that. It is a goal, and nothing less than that, you and I have to reach, if we want to understand what religious life means. If you express your love — nonviolence — in such a manner that it impresses itself indelibly upon your so-called enemy, your enemy must return that love.

—Vol. 13, February 16, 1916

It is no nonviolence if we merely love those who love us. It is nonviolence only when we love those who hate us. I know how difficult it is to follow this grand law of love. But are not all great and good things difficult to do? Love of the hater is the most

difficult of all. But by the grace of God even this most difficult thing becomes easy to accomplish if we want to do it.
— *Selections from Gandhi,* December 31, 1934, 17

The basic principle on which the practice of nonviolence rests is that what holds good in respect of yourself, holds good equally in respect of the whole universe. All humans in essence are alike. What is, therefore, possible for me is possible for everybody. Pursuing further this line of reasoning, I came to the conclusion that if I could find a nonviolent solution of the various problems that arise in one particular village, the lesson learned from it would enable me to tackle in a nonviolent manner all similar problems in India.

In its positive form, nonviolence means the largest love, the greatest charity. If I am a follower of nonviolence, I must love my enemy. I must apply the same rules to the wrong-doer who is my enemy or a stranger to me, as I would to my wrong-doing father or son. This active nonviolence necessarily includes truth and fearlessness. The practice of nonviolence calls forth the greatest courage.

We should try to understand the psychology of evildoers. They are very often victim of their circumstances. By patience and sympathy, we shall be able to win over at least some of them to the side of justice. Moreover, we should not forget that even evil is sustained through the cooperation, either willing or forced, of good people. Truth alone is self-sustained. In the last resort we can curb the power of the evildoers to do mischief by withdrawing all cooperation from them and completely isolating them.

This in essence is the principle of nonviolent noncooperation. It follows, therefore, that it must have its roots in love. Its object should not be to punish the opponents or to inflict injury upon them. Even while noncooperating with them, we must make them feel that in us they have a friend, and we should try to reach their heart by rendering them humanitarian service whenever possible. In fact, it is the acid test of nonviolence that in a nonviolent conflict there is no rancor left behind, and in the end the enemies are converted into friends. That was my experience in South Africa with General Smuts. He started with being my bitterest opponent and critic. Today he is my warmest friend. For eight years we were ranged on opposite sides. But during the Second Round Table Conference it was he who stood by me and, in public as well as in private, gave me his full support. This is only one instance out of many that I can quote.

Times change and systems decay. But it is my faith that in the end, it is only nonviolence and things that are based on nonviolence that will endure. Nineteen hundred years ago, Christianity was born. The ministry of Jesus lasted only for three brief years. His teaching was misunderstood even during his own time, and today's Christianity is a denial of his central teaching, "Love your enemy." But what are nineteen hundred years for the spread of the central doctrine of a person's teaching?

Six centuries rolled by and Islam appeared on the scene. Many Muslims will not even allow me to say that Islam, as the word implies, is unadulterated peace. My reading of the Koran has convinced me that the basis of Islam is not violence. But here again thirteen hundred years are but a speck in the cycle of Time. I am convinced that both these great faiths will live only to the extent that their followers imbibe the central teaching of nonviolence. But it is not a thing to be grasped through mere intellect, it must sink into our hearts.   —Vol. 68, October–November 1938

In the course of serving your fellow creatures you will get a measure of the progress you have made in nonviolence and of the power that is in nonviolence. Armed with this power, a single person can stand against the whole world. That is not possible with the sword.   —Vol. 68, October 1938

My fight continued even when I was lodged behind prison bars. I have been several times in prison, and every time I have left only friends behind in jail, officials and others with whom I have come in contact. It is a specialty of nonviolence that its action never stops. That cannot be said of the sword or the bullet. The bullet can destroy the enemy; nonviolence converts the enemy into a friend and thus enables civil resisters to assimilate to themselves the enemy's strength.   —Vol. 68, October 23, 1938

My study and experience of nonviolence have proved to me that it is the greatest force in the world. It is the surest method of discovering the truth and it is the quickest because there is no other. It works silently, almost imperceptibly, but nonetheless surely. It is the one constructive process of nature in the midst of incessant destruction going on about us. I hold it to be a superstition to believe that it can work only in private life. There is no department of life public or private to which that force cannot be applied. But this nonviolence is impossible without complete self-effacement.
                    —Letter to the Fellowship of Reconciliation-USA,
                              Vol. 25, November 14, 1924

Nonviolence is the greatest force humanity has been endowed with. Truth is the only goal humanity has. For God is none other than Truth. But Truth cannot be and never will be reached except through nonviolence.

   That which distinguishes humanity from all other animals is our capacity to be nonviolent. And humanity fulfills this mission only to the extent that humanity is nonviolent and no more. Humanity has no doubt many other gifts. But if they do not subserve the main purpose — the development of the spirit of nonviolence in humanity — they but drag humanity down lower than the brute, a status from which humanity has only just emerged.

   The cry for peace will be a cry in the wilderness, so long as the spirit of nonviolence does not dominate millions of men and women.   —Message to the Fellowship of Reconciliation-USA,
                          "The Word Tomorrow," October 1926

One person who can express nonviolence in life exercises a force superior to all the forces of brutality.
                         —Nonviolence in Peace and War,
                              Vol. 1, March 14, 1936, 113

Nonviolence in its dynamic condition means conscious suffering. It does not mean meek submission to the will of the evildoer, but it means putting one's whole soul against the will of the tyrant. Working under this law of our being, it is possible for a single individual to defy the whole might of an unjust empire to save his honor, his religion, his soul, and lay the foundation for that empire's fall or regeneration.   —Vol. 18, August 11, 1920

NONVIOLENCE MEANS PURE LOVE

When we claim to be nonviolent, we are expected not to be angry with those who have injured us. We will not wish them harm; we will wish them well; we will not swear at them; we will not cause them any physical hurt. We will put up with all the injury to which we are subjected by the wrongdoers. Thus nonviolence is complete innocence. Complete nonviolence is complete absence of ill will against all that lives. It therefore embraces even sub-human life not excluding noxious insects or beasts. They have not been created to feed our destructive propensities. If we only knew the mind of the Creator, we should find their proper place in God's creation. Nonviolence is therefore, in its active form, goodwill toward all life. It is pure Love. I read it in the Hindu scriptures, in the Bible, in the Koran.

Nonviolence is a perfect state. It is a goal toward which all humanity moves naturally though unconsciously. People do not become divine when they personify innocence in themselves. Only then do they become truly human. In our present state, we are partly human and partly beasts. In our ignorance and even arrogance, we say that we truly fulfill the purpose of our species when we deliver blow for blow and develop the measure of anger required for the purpose. We pretend to believe that retaliation is the law of our being, whereas in every scripture we find that retaliation is nowhere obligatory but only permissible. It is restraint that is obligatory. Restraint is the law of our being. For highest perfection is unattainable without highest restraint. Suffering is thus the badge of the human tribe.

The goal ever recedes from us. The greater the progress, the greater the recognition of our unworthiness. Satisfaction lies in the effort, not in the attainment. Full effort is full victory. Therefore, though I realize more than ever how far I am from that goal, for me the law of complete Love is the law of my being. Each time I fail, my effort shall be all the more determined for my failure.

Our nonviolence need not be of the strong, but it has to be of the truthful. We must not intend harm to the English or to our cooperating compatriots if and while we claim to be nonviolent. But the majority of us have intended harm, and we have refrained from doing it because of our weakness or under the ignorant belief that mere refraining from physical hurt amounted to due fulfillment of our pledge. Our pledge of nonviolence excludes the possibility of future retaliation. Some of us seem, unfortunately, to have merely postponed the date of revenge.

—Vol. 23, March 3, 1922

•

Nonviolence is not merely a negative state of harmlessness, but it is a positive state of love, of doing good even to the evil-doer. But it does not mean helping the evildoer to continue the wrong or tolerating it by passive acquiescence. On the contrary, love — the active state of nonviolence — requires you to resist the wrong-doer by dissociating yourself from him, even though it may offend him.   —Vol. 18, August 25, 1920

Nonviolence means an ocean of compassion. It means shedding from us every trace of ill will for others. It does not mean abjectness or timidity, or fleeing in fear. It means, on the contrary, firmness of mind and courage, a resolute spirit.

Let us resolve that we will never give up the pursuit of truth. To follow truth, the only right path in this world is that of nonviolence. Nonviolence means an ocean of love, whose vastness no one has ever been able to measure. If it fills us we would be so large-hearted that we would have room in it for the whole world. I know this is difficult to achieve, but not impossible. Such nonviolence is not limited to refraining from killing disabled creatures. It may be dharma not to kill them, but love goes infinitely further than that. —Vol. 37, September 16, 1928

•

Nonviolence is a living force. No one has been or will ever be able to measure its limits or its extent. Nonviolence means universal love. It implies compassion for all living beings and the resultant strength to sacrifice oneself. Since many mistakes may be made while this love expresses itself we cannot give up the quest for the whole of this dharma. Even the mistakes committed while seeking the pure path take us a step forward in the quest.
—Vol. 38, November 11, 1928

•

The mouse is not nonviolent toward the cat. At heart, he always has a feeling of violence toward the cat. He cannot kill the latter because he is weak. The person alone has the power to practice the dharma of nonviolence who although fully capable of inflicting violence does not inflict it. That person alone practices the law of nonviolence who voluntarily and with love refrains from inflicting violence on anyone. Nonviolence implies love, compassion, and forgiveness. The Shastras describe these as the virtues of the brave. This courage is not physical but mental. There have been instances of physically frail men and women having indulged in grave acts of violence with the help of others. There have also been cases where physically strong people have granted pardon to kings. Hence, so long as one has not developed inner strength, one can never practice the dharma of nonviolence.

Nonviolence is a great vow. It is more difficult than walking on the edge of a sword. Severe penance is required for its practice. Penance should be taken to mean renunciation and knowledge.

Nonviolence and truth together form, as it were, the right angle of all religions. Those who practice the dharma of nonviolence should increase their inner strength by being always on the alert and progressively restricting the latitude that they have allowed for themselves. There is certainly nothing religious about

indulgence. Renouncing through knowledge the worldly life —
this is the attainment of salvation. Such absolute renunciation is
not to be found even on the peaks of the Himalayas. The true
cave is the one in the heart. People can hide themselves within
it and thus protected can remain untouched by the world even
though living and moving freely in it, taking part in those activities which cannot be avoided.   —Vol. 28, August 9, 1925

•

I believe that the religion of nonviolence springs from the fact
that the advancement of one promotes the advancement of all,
and the fall of one implies the fall of all. We have therefore been
enjoined to show compassion to every living being.
                                    —Vol. 24, August 10, 1927

NONVIOLENCE IS THE WAY
OF TRUTH AND PEACE

The way of peace is the way of truth. Truthfulness is even more
important than peacefulness. Indeed, lying is the mother of violence. Truthful people cannot long remain violent. They will
perceive in the course of their search that they have no need to
be violent and they will further discover that so long as there
is the slightest trace of violence within, they will fail to find the
truth they are seeking.

There is no half way between truth and nonviolence on the
one hand and untruth and violence on the other. We may never
be strong enough to be entirely nonviolent in thought, word, and
deed. But we must keep nonviolence as our goal and make steady
progress toward it. The attainment of freedom, whether for a person, a nation, or the world, must be in exact proportion to the
attainment of nonviolence by each. Let those, therefore, who believe in nonviolence as the only method of achieving real freedom
keep the lamp of nonviolence burning bright in the midst of the
present impenetrable gloom. The truth of a few will count; the

untruth of millions will vanish even like chaff before a whiff of
wind.   —Vol. 30, May 20, 1926

•

If there were no greed, there would be no occasion for armaments. The principle of nonviolence necessitates complete
abstention from exploitation in any form. Immediately, when the
spirit of exploitation is gone, armaments will be felt as an unbearable burden. Real disarmament cannot come unless the nations of
the world cease to exploit one another.

I believe that true democracy can only be an outcome of nonviolence. The structure of a world federation can be raised only
on a foundation of nonviolence, and violence will have to be totally given up in world affairs.   —Vol. 48, December 28, 1931

There are two alternatives before us. The one is that of violence,
the other of nonviolence; the one of physical strength, the other
of soul force; the one of hatred, the other of love; the one of
disorder, the other of peace; one that is demonic, the other Godly.
If we want *swaraj* [independence], we shall have to strive hard
and follow one of these two courses. As they are incompatible
with each other, the fruit, the swaraj that would be secured by
following the one would necessarily be different from that which
would be secured by following the other. In either case the result
will be known as swaraj, but its contents would be different in
the two cases. We shall reap what we sow.
                                   —Vol. 37, September 9, 1928

There is no escape for any of us save through truth and nonviolence. I know that war is wrong. It is an unmitigated evil. I
know too that it has got to go.
                        —*Nonviolence in Peace and War,* Vol. 1,
                                      September 13, 1928, 75

Without nonviolence, it is not possible to seek and find Truth.
Nonviolence and Truth are so intertwined that it is practically
impossible to disentangle and separate them. They are like the

two sides of a coin, or rather a smooth unstamped metallic disc. Who can say, which is the obverse, and which the reverse? Nevertheless, nonviolence is the means, Truth is the end. Means to be means must always be within our reach, and so nonviolence is our supreme duty. If we take care of the means, we are bound to reach the end sooner or later. When once we have grasped this point, final victory is beyond question. Whatever difficulties we encounter, whatever apparent reverses we sustain, we may not give up the quest for Truth which alone is, being God.

—*All Men Are Brothers,* 74

•

My nonviolence is neither maimed nor weak. It is all-powerful. Where there is nonviolence, there is Truth, and Truth is God. How God manifests himself, I cannot say. All I know is that God is all-pervading and where God is, all is well. There is, therefore, one law for all. Wherever in the world Truth and Nonviolence reign supreme, there is peace and happiness. If they are not to be found anywhere we must understand that they are hidden from view. But they cannot totally disappear. Those who possess the bark of this faith, will safely go across in it and carry others across.   —Vol. 85, September 19 and 29, 1946

THE VIRTUE OF NONVIOLENCE

If the dharma of nonviolence is really good, insistence on following it in every way in our daily life is not a mistake, but a duty. There should be no clash between worldly actions and dharma. Action which is opposed to dharma deserves to be eschewed. It is violence and delusion and ignorance to say that nonviolence cannot be practiced at all times, in all places, and fully and so to set it aside. True endeavor consists in seeing that our daily conduct follows nonviolence. This requires real endeavor. Acting thus, we will ultimately gain the supreme state because we will become fit fully to observe nonviolence.   —Vol. 40, March 31, 1929

Nonviolence and cowardice are contradictory terms. Nonviolence is the greatest virtue, cowardice the greatest vice. Nonviolence springs from love, cowardice from hate. Nonviolence always suffers, cowardice would always inflict suffering. Perfect nonviolence is the highest bravery.

—Vol. 42, October 31, 1929

•

I hold that nonviolence is not merely a personal virtue. It is also a social virtue, to be cultivated like the other virtues. Surely, society is largely regulated by the expression of nonviolence in its mutual dealings. What I ask for is an extension of it on a larger, national and international scale.

Though I cannot claim to be a Christian in the sectarian sense, the example of Jesus' suffering is a factor in the composition of my undying faith in nonviolence which rules all my actions, worldly and temporal. And I know that there are hundreds of Christians who believe likewise. Jesus lived and died in vain if he did not teach us to regulate the whole of life by the eternal Law of Love.   —Vol. 68, January 2, 1939

TRAINING IN NONVIOLENCE

If the method of violence takes plenty of training, the method of nonviolence takes even more training, and that training is much more difficult than the training for violence. The first essential of that training is a living faith in God. Those who have a living faith in God will not do evil deeds with the name of God on their lips. Such persons will not rely on the sword, but will rely solely on God. But you may say that cowards may also pass off as believers in God, saying they do not use the sword. Cowardice is no sign of belief in God. The true person of God has the strength to use the sword, but will not use it knowing that every person is the image of God. Only those are people of God who see God in every soul. Such persons would not be prepared to kill another.

Nonviolence is meant for all irrespective of faith. As votaries of nonviolence, we will forget violence.

True nonviolence is mightier than the mightiest violence. If you really know the essential nature of nonviolence, you will have to pledge yourselves to nonviolence, and that in spite of the fact that violence is so much in the air and we are talking day in and day out of military maneuvers and aerial action, armaments and naval strength. You have to realize that the power of unarmed nonviolence is any day far superior to that of armed force. With me acceptance of nonviolence was instinctive. It was part of my training and home influence in childhood. I have been preaching the creed of nonviolence for fifty years. Its superior strength I came to realize in South Africa where I had to pit it against organized violence and racial prejudice. I practiced it in South Africa, where everybody is armed and the government has introduced conscription. I returned from South Africa with clear conviction of the superiority of the method of nonviolence to that of violence. In India also, we have used it for gaining our rights, and we have achieved some measure of success.

—Vol. 67, May 4 and 14, 1938

If you really want to cultivate nonviolence, you should take a pledge that, come what may, you will not give way to anger or order about members of your household or lord it over them. You can thus utilize trifling little occasions in everyday life to cultivate nonviolence in your own person and teach it to your children.   —Vol. 67, January 7, 1939

•

Just as one must learn the art of killing in the training of violence, so one must learn the art of dying in the training for nonviolence. Nonviolence has no cause for fear. Votaries of nonviolence have to cultivate the capacity for sacrifice of the highest type in order to be free from fear. They worry not if they should lose their land, their wealth, their life. Those who have not overcome all fear cannot practice nonviolence to perfection. Votaries of nonviolence have only one fear, that is of God. Those who seek refuge in God ought to have a glimpse of the soul that transcends the body, and the moment one has a glimpse of the imperishable soul, one sheds the love of the perishable body. Training in nonviolence is thus diametrically opposed to training in violence. Violence is needed for the protection of things external. Nonviolence is needed for the protection of the soul, for the protection of one's honor.

This nonviolence cannot be learned by staying at home. It needs enterprise. In order to test ourselves, we should learn to dare danger and death, to mortify the flesh, and to acquire the capacity to endure all manner of hardships. Those who tremble or take to their heels the moment they see two people fighting are not nonviolent, but cowards. Nonviolent persons will lay down their lives in preventing such quarrels. The bravery of the non-violent is vastly superior to that of the violent. The badge of the violent is their weapon — a spear, sword, or rifle. God is the shield of the nonviolent.

It will be evident from the foregoing that there is no compar-ison between the two types of bravery. The one is limited, the other is limitless. There is no such thing as out-daring or out-fighting nonviolence. Nonviolence is invincible. There need be no doubt that this nonviolence can be achieved.

—Vol. 72, August 27, 1940

•

The way of nonviolence and truth is as sharp as the razor's edge. Its practice is more than our daily food. Rightly taken, food sus-tains the body; rightly practiced, nonviolence sustains the soul. The body food we can only take in measured quantities and at stated intervals; nonviolence, which is spiritual food, we have to take continually. There is no such thing as inaction. I have to be conscious every moment that I am pursuing the goal, and have to examine myself in terms of that goal.   —Vol. 67, April 2, 1938

Your nonviolence must shine through your speech, your action, your general behavior. A votary of nonviolence must cultivate a habit of unremitting toil, sleepless vigilance, ceaseless self-control.

—Vol. 69, May 6, 1939

Nonviolence magnifies one's own defects and minimizes those of the opponent. It regards the mote in one's own eye as a beam, and the beam in the opponent's eye as a mote.

—Vol. 69, May 13, 1939

Nonviolence is not like a garment to be put on and off at will. Its seat is in the heart and it must be an inseparable part of our very being.   —Vol. 31, August 12, 1926

●

Nonviolence to be a creed has to be all-pervasive. I cannot be nonviolent about one activity of mine and violent about others. That would be a policy, not a life-force. Let me lay down five simple axioms of nonviolence as I know it:

1. Nonviolence implies as complete self-purification as is humanly possible.

2. Person for person, the strength of nonviolence is in exact proportion to the ability, not the will, of the nonviolent person to inflict violence.

3. Nonviolence is without exception superior to violence. The power at the disposal of nonviolent persons is always greater than they would have if they were violent.

4. There is no such thing as defeat in nonviolence. The end of violence is surest defeat.

5. The ultimate end of nonviolence is surest victory, if such a term may be used of nonviolence. In reality where there is no sense of defeat, there is no sense of victory.

—Vol. 62, February 1936

●

Nonviolence succeeds only when we have a living faith in God.

—Vol. 68, January 28, 1939

The acid test of nonviolence is that one thinks, speaks, and acts nonviolently, even when there is the gravest provocation to be violent. There is no merit in being nonviolent to the good and the gentle. Nonviolence is the mightiest force in the world capable of resisting the greatest imaginable temptation. Jesus knew "the generation of vipers," minced no words in describing them, but pleaded for mercy for them before the judgment throne, "for they knew not what they were doing."

—Vol. 64, December 19, 1936

•

How are we to train individuals or communities in this difficult art of nonviolence? There is no royal road, except through living the creed in your life which must be a living sermon. Of course, the expression in one's own life presupposes great study, tremendous perseverance, and thorough cleansing of one's self of all the impurities. If for mastering of the physical sciences you have to devote a whole lifetime, how many lifetimes may be needed for mastering the greatest spiritual force that humanity has known? But why worry even if it means several lifetimes? For, if this is the only permanent thing in life, if this is the only thing that counts, then whatever effort you bestow on mastering it is well spent. Seek ye first the Kingdom of Heaven and everything else shall be added unto you. The Kingdom of Heaven is nonviolence.

—Vol. 62, March 14, 1936

•

We bow to Mother Earth every morning and pray for her forgiveness for touching her with our feet. The Earth bears our burden but does not hurt us; she bears the burden uncomplainingly. According to modern discoveries, she is hanging in space without support. If she were to get angry with us and stray ever so slightly from her path, we would instantly perish. For thousands of years, however, the earth has been rotating in her orbit and has sustained our life. This is the utmost limit of humility. We have sprung from this earth and to that shall we return. After knowing this, what pride can we feel? We are but a particle of dust and should remain so.

Those who wish to kick us or insult us should be welcome to do so; such is the humility which nonviolence implies. Cultivate it and you will be able to dance with joy.

—Vol. 47, July 30, 1931

•

When you take up the weapon of satyagraha, you prepare yourself to face without retaliation the gravest danger and provocation. It gives you a chance to surrender your life for the cause when the time comes. To be able to do so nonviolently requires previous training. If you are a believer in the orthodox method [of war] you go and train yourselves as soldiers. It is the same with nonviolence. You have to alter your whole mode of life and work for it in peace time just as much as in the time of war. It is no doubt a difficult job. You have to put your whole soul into it; and if you are sincere, your example will affect the lives of other people around you. America is today exploiting the so-called weaker nations of the world along with other powers. It has become the richest country in the world, not a thing to be proud of when we come to think of the means by which she has become rich. Again, to protect these riches you need the assistance of violence. You must be prepared to give up these riches. Therefore, if you really mean to give up violence, you will say, "We shall have nothing to do with the spoils of violence, and if as a result America ceases to be rich, we do not mind." You will then be qualified to offer a spotless sacrifice. That is the meaning of preparation. The occasion for making the extreme sacrifice may not come if you as a nation have fully learned to live for peace. It is much more difficult to live for nonviolence than to die for it.

Nonviolence is love in essence. But perhaps "love" does not express my meaning fully. The nearest word is "charity." We love our friends and our equals. But the reaction that a ruthless dictator sets up in us is either that of awe or pity according respectively as we react to him violently or nonviolently. Nonviolence knows no fear. If I am truly nonviolent, I would pity the dictator and say to myself, "He does not know what a human being should be. One day he will know better when he is confronted by a people who do not stand in awe of him, who will neither submit nor cringe to him, nor bear any grudge against him for whatever he may do." Germans are today doing what they are doing because all the other nations stand in awe of them. None of them can go to Hitler with clean hands.

— Vol. 68, interview with American teachers,
December 29, 1938

•

Unless we kindle the flame of unadulterated nonviolence and truth within ourselves we shall not realize our goal of complete independence. With that light kindled within us, the tendency toward violence will automatically vanish and riots will be brought under control. Just as in training for violence one learns to kill, similarly in adopting nonviolence, one should learn the art of dying. There is no place at all for fear in nonviolence. Not only that, one has to develop the spirit of sacrifice to such a high degree that one would not hesitate to sacrifice one's family, property, and even one's life. A votary of nonviolence should fear God alone. One resorts to violence to protect one's physical body. But we should realize that the body is perishable and it is the soul which really matters. And in order to protect the honor of one's soul there is no alternative to nonviolence.

There is no school where such nonviolence can be taught. Our nonviolence is tested only when we act with courage. Truly nonviolent persons should brave the danger and prove their worth. The courage of a nonviolent person is many times superior to the courage of a violent person. But who listens to me? I do, however, hope to meet death, if anyone should come to kill me, without a trace of anger, calmly, with a smile, and all the while remembering my chosen God. I believe that God will grant me this strength. I am growing daily stronger in my conviction that God will bless me with a death befitting a nonviolent person.

— Vol. 87, May 4, 1947

•

A nonviolent body will have no use for weapons and will therefore beat its swords into plowshares and spears into pruning hooks, and will shrink from the thought of using them as lethal weapons. The violent soldier will be trained in the use of violence by being taught to shoot. The nonviolent soldier will have no time for this pastime. Nonviolent persons will get all their training through nursing the sick, saving those in danger at the risk of their own life, patrolling places which may be in fear of thieves and rioters, and in laying down their lives, if necessary, in dissuading them from their purpose. The first and last shield and buckler of nonviolent persons will be their unwavering faith in God.

In the dictionary of nonviolence, there is no such word as "enemy." Even for the supposed enemy, nonviolent persons will have nothing but compassion in their heart. They will believe that no one is intentionally wicked, that there is no person but is gifted with the faculty to discriminate between right and wrong, and that if that faculty were to be fully developed, it would surely mature into nonviolence. They will therefore pray to God that God may give the supposed enemy a sense of right and bless that person. Their prayer for themselves will always be that the spring of compassion in them may ever be flowing and that they may ever grow in moral strength so that they may face death fearlessly.

—Vol. 73, February 15, 1941

NONVIOLENCE IS THE RULE OF LIFE

For me, nonviolence is not a mere philosophical principle. It is the rule and breath of my life. I know I fail often, sometimes consciously, more often unconsciously. It is a matter not of the intellect but of the heart.   —Vol. 37, September 13, 1928

The basic principle on which the practice of nonviolence rests is that what holds good in respect of oneself equally applies to the whole universe.   —Vol. 68, November 12, 1938

Nonviolence is a matter of the heart. It does not come to us through any intellectual feat. We all have faith in God though we all do not know it. For we all have faith in ourselves and that multiplied to the nth degree is God. The sum total of all that lives is God. We may not be God, but we are of God, even as a little drop of water is of the ocean. Imagine it torn away from the ocean and flung millions of miles away. It becomes helpless torn from its surroundings, and cannot feel the might and majesty of the ocean. But if someone could point out to it that it is of the ocean, its faith would revive, it would dance with joy, and the whole of the might and majesty of the ocean would be reflected in it. Even so it is with all nonviolent activities.

—Vol. 70, June 3, 1939

Nonviolence alone is the true religion for all times. Nonviolence is the dharma of awakening. Its votary has to make conscious use of it at every moment as we are surrounded by violence on all sides. Every one of us has according to our capacity to make our own way out of this dangerous predicament.

—Vol. 61, July 28, 1935

•

Here are the implications and conditions of nonviolence:

1. Nonviolence is the law of the human race. It is infinitely greater than and superior to brute force.

2. In the last resort it does not avail to those who do not possess a living faith in the God of love.

3. Nonviolence affords the fullest protection to one's self-respect and sense of honor, but not always to possession of land or movable property, though its habitual practice does prove a better bulwark than the possession of armed men to defend them. Nonviolence in the very nature of things is of no assistance in the defense of ill-gotten gains and immoral acts.

4. Individuals or nations who would practice nonviolence must be prepared to sacrifice (nations to the last person) their all except honor. It is therefore inconsistent with the possession of other people's countries, i.e., modern imperialism, which is frankly based on military force for its defense.

5. Nonviolence is a power which can be wielded equally by all — children, young men and women, or grown-up people — provided they have a living faith in the God of love and have therefore equal love for all humankind. When nonviolence is accepted as the law of life it must pervade the whole being and not be applied to isolated acts.

6. It is a profound error to suppose that while the law is good enough for individuals, it is not for masses of humanity.

—Vol. 63, September 5, 1936

•

Nonviolence cannot be divided into compartments. Nonviolence is an inherent attribute of humanity or, at any rate, it should be an attribute of humanity during waking hours. Devotion to nonviolence is the highest expression of humanity's conscious state. If we thus conceive nonviolence, we should satisfy all our necessities by the labor of our hands. If we do not do this, we shall have to depend upon other powers and as long as such condition persists, we shall be unable to realize a state of fearlessness.

—Vol. 82, November 28, 1945

NONVIOLENCE CAN BE
PRACTICED BY NATIONS

We have to make truth and nonviolence not matters for mere individual practice, but for practice by groups and communities and nations. That, at any rate, is my dream. I shall live and die in trying to realize it. My faith helps me to discover new

truths every day. Nonviolence is the attribute of the soul, and therefore to be practiced by everybody in all the affairs of life.
—Vol. 71, March 2, 1940

If one person can practice nonviolence, surely a nation can. No person or group of people can hold any other person or group of people slaves against their will. The slave-driver will say "Do this" and they will refuse. It is possible to imagine that some day all nations will become sufficiently intelligent to act, even in the mass, as individuals do today.   —Vol. 66, September 9, 1939

Just as violence has its own technique, known by the military, which has invented means of destruction unheard of before, nonviolence has its own science and technique. Nonviolence in politics is a new weapon in the process of evolution. Its vast possibilities are yet unexplored. The exploration can take place only if it is practiced on a big scale and in various fields.
—Vol. 66, October 23, 1937

•

You know that even a society based on violence functions only with the help of experts. We want to bring about a new social order based on truth and nonviolence. We need experts to develop this into a science. The world as it functions today represents a mixture of violence and nonviolence. The external surface of the world suggests its internal state. A country like Germany which regards violence as God is engaged only in developing violence and glorifying it. We are watching the efforts that the votaries of violence are making. We must also know that those given to violence are watching our activities. They are observing what we are doing for developing our science.

But the way of violence is old and established. It is not so difficult to do research in it. The way of nonviolence is new. The science of nonviolence is yet taking shape. We are still not conversant with all its aspects. There is a wide scope for research and experiment in this field. You can apply all your talents to it.

For me, nonviolence is something to be shunned if it is a private virtue. My concept of nonviolence is universal. It belongs to the millions. I am here just to serve them. Anything that cannot reach the millions is not for me. It should be so for my colleagues as well. We were born to prove that truth and nonviolence are not just rules for personal conduct. They can become the policy of a group, a community, a nation. We have not yet proved this, but that alone can be the aim of our life. I have regarded this alone as my duty. I shall not leave it even if the whole world abandons me. So profound is my faith. I would live only to attain this and die only in that endeavor. My faith gives me new visions every day. Today I am seeing ever new miracles of nonviolence. Every day I have a new vision and I experience a new joy. I am certain that nonviolence is meant for all time. It is an attribute of the soul and is therefore universal since the soul belongs to all. Nonviolence is meant for everybody and for all time and at all places. If it is really an attribute of the soul, it should be inherent in us.   — Vol. 71, April 8, 1940

•

I would say to any who would assault me that they may destroy my home and hearth, why, even my person, but they would not be able to destroy my soul. I would not defend my country with foreign arms. If I could have my say I would place in the hands of the police hoe and spade instead of bayonets so that they could take to farming. Besides, a country wedded to nonviolence is not bothered about foreign aggression because all its citizens will be prepared to lay down their life. It is my belief that nonviolence is not an entirely personal quality. It is an easy way of spiritual as well as political action for all — for the individual, for society, and for country.

— Vol. 87, April 4, 1947

•

For nonviolence to permeate us we should have a living faith in God. Nonviolence comes to us through doing good continually without the slightest expectation of return. It simply spends itself and it is its own reward, and done in that spirit. It is done not merely for friends but certainly for adversaries. That is the indispensable lesson in nonviolence. It was thrown my way by God in South Africa in an atmosphere which was as adverse as it well could be. I was in a country where I knew no European or Indian. I had gone there to make a career as a lawyer. But I succeeded in learning the eternal law of suffering as the only remedy for undoing wrong and injustice. It means positively the law of nonviolence. You have to be prepared to suffer cheerfully at the hands of all and sundry, and you will wish ill to no one, not even to those who may have wronged you.

Just now a good many people are talking of world peace, promoting peace societies and passing resolutions. This is good as far as it goes. But it may not be nonviolence. An army of nonviolence exposes itself to all the risks that an army of violence does. Only the latter expects to retaliate even when it is not the aggressor. An army of nonviolence runs risks without the wish to retaliate.

I am not enamored of numbers. A peace army does not rely upon numbers unless they understand the implications of nonviolence. I would, therefore, concentrate on a few becoming saturated with the spirit of nonviolence and disciplining themselves for the utmost suffering.

How exactly to act in particular situations is a matter of waiting on God. The answer comes straight in response to prayer from the heart. Such prayer carries with it the anguish of the soul.
— Vol. 66, March 12, 1938

•

Democracy and violence can ill go together. The nations that are today nominally democratic have either to become frankly totalitarian or, if they are to become truly democratic, they must become courageously nonviolent. It is a blasphemy to say that nonviolence can be practiced only by individuals and never by nations which are composed of individuals.
— Vol. 68, November 5, 1938

MY EXPERIENCE OF NONVIOLENCE

I have been practicing with scientific precision nonviolence and its possibilities for an unbroken period of over fifty years. I have applied it in every walk of life — domestic, institutional, economic, and political. I know of no single case in which it has failed. Where it has seemed sometimes to have failed, I have ascribed it to my imperfections. I claim no perfection for myself. But I do claim to be a passionate seeker after Truth, which is but another name for God. In the course of that search, the discovery of nonviolence came to me. Its spread is my life mission. I have no interest in living except for the prosecution of that mission.
— Selected Works, Vol. 6, July 6, 1940, 163

There is that difference between a belief in nonviolence and a belief in violence which there is between north and south, and life and death. Those who hook their fortunes to nonviolence, the law of love, daily lessen the circle of destruction and to that extent promote life and love. Those who swear by violence, the law of hate, daily widen the circle of destruction and to that extent promote death and hate. I [have] preached without adulteration the grand doctrine of the eternal Law of Love of all life. Though I may fail to carry it out to the full in this life, my faith in it shall abide. Every failure brings me nearer the realization.
— Vol. 61, June 22, 1935

•

My faith in nonviolence remains as strong as ever. I am quite sure that not only should it answer all our requirements in our country, but that it should, if properly applied, prevent the bloodshed that is going on outside India and is threatening to overwhelm the Western world. My aspiration is limited. God has not given me the power to guide the world on the path of nonviolence. But I have imagined that God has chosen me as God's instrument for presenting nonviolence to India for dealing with her many ills. The progress already made is great. But much more remains to be done. I do entertain the hope that there is yet work for me to do, that the darkness that seems to have enveloped me will disappear, and that, whether with another battle more brilliant than the Dandi Salt March, India will come to her own demonstrably through nonviolent means. I am praying for the light that will dispel the darkness. Let those who have a living faith in nonviolence join me in the prayer. —Vol. 67, July 23, 1938

•

In my opinion, nonviolence is not passivity in any shape or form. Nonviolence, as I understand it, is the most active force in the world. Therefore, whether it is materialism or anything else, if nonviolence does not provide an effective antidote, it is not the active force of my conception. Or, to put it conversely, if you bring me some conundrums that I cannot answer I would say my nonviolence is still defective. Nonviolence is the supreme law. During my half a century of experience I have not yet come across a situation when I had to say that I was helpless, that I had no remedy in terms of nonviolence.

Take the question of the Jews. Jews need not feel helpless [against Nazi Germany] if they take to the nonviolent way. A friend has written me a letter objecting that in that article I have assumed that the Jews have been violent. It is true that the Jews have not been actively violent in their own persons. But they called down upon the Germans the curses of humanity, and they wanted America and England to fight Germany on their behalf. If I hit my adversaries, that is of course violence, but to be truly nonviolent, I must love them and pray for them even when they hit me. The Jews have not been actively nonviolent or, in spite of the misdeeds of the dictators, they would say, "We shall suffer at their hands; they knew no better. But we shall suffer not in the manner in which they want us to suffer." If even one Jew acted thus, he or she would save his or her self-respect and leave an example which, if it became infectious, would save the whole of Judaism and leave a rich heritage to humanity besides.

Those who rain death from above have never any chance of even knowing who and how many they have killed. How can nonviolence combat aerial warfare, seeing that there are no personal contacts? The reply to this is that behind the death-dealing bomb there is the human hand that releases it, and behind that still, is the human heart that sets the hand in motion. And at the back of the policy of terrorism is the assumption that terrorism if applied in a sufficient measure will produce the desired result, namely, bend the adversary to the tyrant's will. But supposing a people make up their mind that they will never do the tyrant's will, nor retaliate with the tyrant's own methods, the tyrant will not find it worth his while to go on with his terrorism. If sufficient food is given to the tyrant, a time will come when he will have had more than enough. If all the mice in the world held a conference together and resolved that they would no more fear the cat but all run into her mouth, the mice would live. I have actually seen a cat play with a mouse. She did not kill it outright but held it between her jaws, then released it, and again pounced upon it as soon as it made an effort to escape. In the end, the mouse died out of sheer fright. The cat would have derived no sport if the mouse had not tried to run away. I learned the lesson of nonviolence from my wife when I tried to bend her to my will. Her determined resistance to my will on the one hand, and her quiet submission to the suffering my stupidity involved on the other, ultimately made me ashamed of myself and cured me of my stupidity in thinking that I was born to rule over her, and in the end she became my teacher in nonviolence. And what I did in South Africa was but an extension of the rule of satyagraha which she unwillingly practiced in her own person.

[The current] argument presupposes that dictators like Mussolini or Hitler are beyond redemption. But belief in nonviolence is based on the assumption that human nature in its essence is one and therefore unfailingly responds to the advances of love. It should be remembered that they have up to now always found ready response to the violence that they have used. Within their experience, they have not come across organized nonviolent resistance on an appreciable scale, if at all. Therefore, it is not only highly likely, but I hold it to be inevitable, that they would recognize the superiority of nonviolent resistance over any display of violence that they may be capable of putting forth. Moreover the nonviolent technique that I have presented to the Czechs does not depend for its success on the goodwill of the dictators, for nonviolent resisters depend upon the unfailing assistance of God which sustains them throughout difficulties which would otherwise be considered insurmountable. Their faith makes them indomitable.

You as a Christian can make an effective contribution by nonviolent action even though it may cost you your all. Peace will never come until the Great Powers courageously decide to disarm themselves. I have an implicit faith — faith that today burns brighter than ever, after half a century's experience of unbroken practice of nonviolence — that humanity can only be saved through nonviolence, which is the central teaching of the Bible as I have understood the Bible. — Vol. 68, December 24, 1938

•

If one does not practice nonviolence in one's personal relations with others and hopes to use it in bigger affairs, one is vastly mistaken. Nonviolence like charity must begin at home. But if it is necessary for the individual to be trained in nonviolence, it is even more necessary for the nation to be trained likewise. One cannot be nonviolent in one's own circle and violent outside it. Or else, one is not truly nonviolent even in one's own circle; often the nonviolence is only in appearance. It is only when you meet with resistance, as for instance when a thief or murderer appears, that your nonviolence is put on trial. You either try or should try to oppose the thief with his own weapons, or you try to disarm him by love. Living among decent people, your conduct may not be described as nonviolent. Mutual forbearance is not nonviolence. Immediately, therefore, you get the conviction that nonviolence is the law of life, you have to practice it toward those who act violently toward you, and the law must apply to nations as to individuals. Training is no doubt necessary. And beginnings are always small. But if the conviction is there, the rest will follow.

If one has that pride and egoism, there is no nonviolence. Nonviolence is not possible without humility. My own experience is that whenever I have acted nonviolently I have been led to it and sustained in it by the higher promptings of an unseen Power. Through my own will I should have miserably failed. When I first went to jail, I quailed at the prospect. I had heard terrible things about jail life. But I had faith in God's protection. Our experience was that those who went to jail in a prayerful spirit came out victorious. Those who had gone in their own strength failed. There is no room for self-pitying in it either, when you say God is giving you the strength. Self-pity comes when you do a thing for which you expect recognition from others. But here there is no question of recognition.

Nonviolence is a very slow process, you will perhaps say. Yes, possibly, under the existing adverse circumstances to begin with. But it will gather momentum and speed in an incalculable manner as you proceed. I am an irrepressible optimist. My optimism rests on my belief in the infinite possibilities of the individual to develop nonviolence. The more you develop it in your own being, the more infectious it becomes till it overwhelms your surroundings and by and by might oversweep the world.

Nonviolence succeeds only when we have a living faith in God. Buddha, Jesus, Mohammed — they were all warriors of peace in their own style. We have to enrich the heritage left by these world teachers. God has God's own wonderful way of executing God's plans and choosing God's instruments. All the world teachers, you should know, began with a zero!

—Vol. 68, January 28, 1939

•

The one who has no belief in the constructive program has, in my opinion, no concrete feeling for the starved millions. The one who is devoid of that feeling cannot fight nonviolently. In actual practice the expansion of my nonviolence has kept exact pace with that of my identification with starved humanity.

—Vol. 76, April 12, 1942

•

Our goal is truth, and truth can be reached only through the observance of nonviolence. Nonviolence is only a means. Speaking truth is a habit I have formed right from my childhood, but I had to make efforts to practice nonviolence. If we adopt nonviolence, truth can be followed along with it. Human experience is that as good comes out of good, only evil comes out of evil. Retaliation cannot end violence. If humanity is to rise above violence there is no alternative but to adopt nonviolence. Love alone can conquer hatred. The principles of truth and nonviolence are nothing new. They have been in existence from the beginning of creation. After sixty years' experience, my faith in these ideals is growing stronger day after day.   —Vol. 87, April 18, 1947

NONVIOLENCE BELONGS TO THE BRAVE

Humanity is at the crossroads. It has to make its choice between the law of the jungle and the law of humanity. We in India deliberately adopted the latter twenty-five years back, but I am afraid that while we profess to follow the higher way, our practice has not always conformed to our profession. We have always proclaimed from the house-tops that nonviolence is the way of the brave, but there are some among us who have brought nonviolence into disrepute by using it as a weapon of the weak. Let me say in all humility that nonviolence belongs to the brave. A Gujarati poet has sung: "The way of the Lord is for the brave, not for the coward." By the way of the Lord is here meant the way of nonviolence and truth. I have said before that I do not envisage God other than truth and nonviolence. Nonviolence calls for the strength and courage to suffer without retaliation, to receive blows without returning any. But that does not exhaust its meaning. We have to cultivate that courage. It is an ideal worth living for and dying for.   —Vol. 83, April 4, 1946

•

Nonviolence is not a cloistered virtue confined only to the seer and the cave-dweller. It is capable of being practiced by the millions, not with full knowledge of its implications, but because it is the law of our species. It distinguishes humanity from the brute. But humanity has not shed the brute within. Humanity has to strive to do. This striving applies to the practice of nonviolence, not to the belief in it. I cannot strive to believe in a principle: I either believe in it or I do not. And if I believe in it, I must bravely strive to practice it. Nonviolence is an attribute of the brave. Cowardice and nonviolence do not go together any more than water and fire.   —Vol. 70, November 4, 1939

•

The virtues of mercy, nonviolence, love, and truth in any one can be truly tested only when they are pitted against ruthlessness, violence, hate, and untruth.

If this is true, then it is incorrect to say that nonviolence is of no avail before a murderer. It can certainly be said that to experiment with nonviolence in the face of a murderer is to seek self-destruction. But this is the real test of nonviolence. Those who get themselves killed out of sheer helplessness, however, can in no wise be said to have passed the test. Those who when being killed bear no anger against their murderers and even ask God to forgive them are truly nonviolent. History relates this of Jesus Christ. With his dying breath on the cross, he is reported to have said: "Father, forgive them for they know not what they do." It is another matter that our nonviolence has not reached such heights. It would be wholly wrong for us to lower the standard of nonviolence by reason of our own frailty or lack of experience. Without true understanding of the ideal, we can never hope to reach it. It is necessary for us, therefore, to apply our reason to understand the power of nonviolence.

—Vol. 84, April 21, 1946

•

Hitlers will come and go. Those who believe that when Hitler dies or is defeated his spirit will die, err grievously. What matters is how we react to such a spirit, violently or nonviolently. If we react violently, we feed that evil spirit. If we act nonviolently, we sterilize it.

The great beauty of nonviolent effort lies in the fact that its failure can only harm those who are in it, while its success is sure to promote all-around good.   —Vol. 73, February 15, 1940

•

Nonviolence is a weapon of matchless potency. It is the *summum bonum* of life. It is an attribute of the brave; in fact, it is their all. It does not come within reach of the coward. It is no wooden or lifeless dogma, but a living and a life-giving force. It is the special attribute of the soul. That is why it has been described as the highest dharma, the highest law. In the hands of the educationist, therefore, it ought to take the form of the purest love, ever fresh, an ever gushing spring of life expressing itself in every act. Ill will cannot stand in its presence. The sun of nonviolence carries all the hosts of darkness such as hatred, anger, and malice before itself. Nonviolence in education shines clear and far and can no more be hidden, even as the sun cannot be hidden by any means.
                                            —Vol. 37, September 6, 1928

THE AMAZING DISCOVERIES OF NONVIOLENCE TO COME

We are constantly being astonished these days at the amazing discoveries in the field of violence. But I maintain that far more undreamt of and seemingly impossible discoveries will be made in the field of nonviolence.   —Vol. 72, August 19, 1940

GANDHI'S PRAYER FOR ALL

Nonviolent persons automatically become servants of God. Nonviolent persons should be ready to render account to God of every minute of their time. May you all be true servants of God and true practitioners of nonviolence.   —Vol. 67, May 21, 1938

5

The Discipline of
Prayer and Fasting

"Mute prayer is my greatest weapon," Gandhi once said. Just as the modern world has never known a saint given over to a political struggle for independence, so too the modern world has never known a politician and revolutionary so personally dedicated to the spiritual disciplines of prayer and fasting in pursuit of sanctity. Underlying Gandhi's struggle for racial equality and civil rights in South Africa and political independence and social justice in India lay a lifelong commitment to the spiritual life.

In many ways, Gandhi was, first and foremost, a person of contemplative prayer. For nearly fifty years, he got up early in the morning (usually at 2:00 or 3:00 a.m.) and meditated for one hour, and meditated again for one hour each evening. He read from the scriptures every single day, always from the Bhagavad Gita, but often also from the Sermon on the Mount and the Koran as well. And he undertook eleven public fasts to end violence and injustice and to grow spiritually.

Gandhi insisted over and over that if we are serious in our pursuit of truth and practice of nonviolence we must pray, fast, and discipline ourselves through daily renunciation and self-denial. "The first and the last thing we have to attend to is to reform ourselves," Gandhi wrote. "We must make prayer the center of our days." Without prayer, he realized, we cannot know peace within ourselves, much less be able to practice non-

violence toward those around us as well as our adversaries or be able to lay down our lives in the struggle for justice and peace. "In spite of despair staring me in the face on the political horizon, I have never lost my peace. In fact I have found people who envy my peace. That peace, I tell you, comes from prayer. I am not a man of learning, but I humbly claim to be a man of prayer."

Gandhi regularly wrote and spoke about the discipline of prayer, fasting, humility, and other virtues. During the last few years of his life, he spoke on prayer almost every evening at his daily public prayer service. Gandhi urged everyone to put these spiritual disciplines into practice in our own day-to-day lives and discover, with Gandhi, the self-realization of seeing God face to face.

"I can give my own testimony and say that a heartfelt prayer is undoubtedly the most potent instrument that humanity possesses for overcoming cowardice and all other bad old habits," Gandhi said. "I have never found God lacking in response. I have found God nearest at hand when the horizon seemed darkest — in my ordeals in jails when it was not all smooth sailing for me. I cannot recall a moment in my life when I had a sense of desertion by God."

"When I was in South Africa, I used to pray privately," Gandhi said shortly before his death. "When I returned to India, I saw the necessity of holding mass prayer gatherings. I have been holding them ever since. There is still of course the necessity of individual prayer. Our prayer today to God is to lead us from darkness to light, from untruth to truth, from war to peace, peace not only for India but for the entire world."

PRAYER IS THE CORE OF LIFE

I believe that prayer is the very soul and essence of religion, and therefore prayer must be the very core of the life of humanity, for no one can live without religion. There are some who in the egotism of their reason declare that they have nothing to do with religion. But it is like a person saying that he breathes but that he has no nose. Whether by reason, or by instinct, or by superstition, humanity acknowledges some sort of relationship with the divine.

Prayer is the very core of life. Prayer is either petitional or in its wider sense is inward communion. In either case, the ultimate result is the same. Even when it is petitional, the petition should be for the cleansing and purification of the soul, for freeing it from the layers of ignorance and darkness that envelope it. The one who hungers for the awakening of the divine within must fall back on prayer. But prayer is no mere exercise of words or of the ears; it is no mere repetition of empty formula. Any amount of repetition of God's name is futile if it fails to stir the soul. It is better in prayer to have a heart without words than words without a heart. It must be in clear response to the spirit which hungers for it. And even as a hungry person relishes a hearty meal, a hungry soul will relish a heart-felt prayer. Without prayer there is no inner peace.

We are born to serve our fellow men and women, and we cannot properly do so unless we are wide awake. There is an eternal struggle raging in humanity's breast between the powers of darkness and of light, and the one who has not the anchor of prayer to rely upon will be victim to the powers of darkness. Persons of prayer will be at peace with themselves and with the whole world. Those who go about the affairs of the world without a prayerful heart will be miserable and will make the world also miserable. Apart therefore from its bearing on humanity's condition after death, prayer has incalculable value for humanity in this world of the living. Prayer is the only means of bringing orderliness and peace and repose in our daily acts.

Begin therefore your day with prayer, and make it so soulful that it may remain with you until the evening. Close the day with prayer so that you may have a peaceful night free from dreams and nightmares. Do not worry about the form of prayer. Let it be any form; it should be such as can put us into communion with the divine. Only, whatever be the form, let not the spirit wander while the words of prayer run on out of your mouth.

You whose mission in life is service of your fellow men and

women will go to pieces if you do not impose on yourselves some sort of discipline, and prayer is necessary spiritual discipline. It is discipline and restraint that separates us from the brute. If we want to be men and women walking with our heads erect and not walking on all fours, let us understand and put ourselves under voluntary discipline and restraint.

—Vol. 42, January 23, 1930

•

Prayer is not an old woman's idle amusement. Properly understood and applied, it is the most potent instrument of action. Let us then pray and find out what we have meant by nonviolence and how we shall retain the freedom gained by its use.

—Vol. 83, April 6, 1946

•

If God is, it is our duty to worship God even if we recognize God as Truth. We tend to become what we worship. That is the whole and comprehensive meaning of prayer. Truth abides in the human heart. But we realize it indifferently or not at all. Sincere prayer is the key to such realization.

—*Selected Works,* Vol. 5, June 13, 1932, 35

THY WILL BE DONE

There is really only one prayer that we may offer: "Thy will be done." Someone will ask where is the sense in offering such a prayer. The answer is: Prayer should not be understood in a gross sense. We are aware of the presence of God in our heart, and in order to shake off attachment, we for the moment think of God as different from ourselves and pray to God. That is to say, we do not wish to go where our wayward will may lead us but where the Lord takes us. We do not know whether it is good to live or to die. Therefore we should not take delight in living, nor should we tremble at the thought of death. We should be equally minded toward both. This is the ideal. It may be long before we reach it, and only a few of us can attain it. Even then we must keep it constantly in view, and the more difficult it seems of attainment, the greater should be the effort we put forth.

—*Selected Works,* Vol. 5, May 19, 1932, 378

PRAYER IS A LONGING FOR GOD

Prayer is not an asking. It is a longing of the soul. It is a daily admission of one's weakness. The tallest among us has a perpetual reminder of his nothingness before death, disease, old age, accidents, etc. We are living in the midst of death. What is the value of "working for our own schemes" when they might be reduced to nothing in the twinkling of an eye, or when we may be equally swiftly and unaware be taken away from them? But we may feel strong as a rock, if we could truthfully say, "We work for God and God's schemes." Then all is as clear as daylight. Then nothing perishes. All perishing is then only what seems. Death and destruction have "then, but only then," no reality about them. For death or destruction is then but a change. An artist destroys his picture for creating a better one. A watchmaker throws away a bad spring to put in a new and useful one.

—Vol. 31, September 23, 1926

•

Prayer is an intense longing to have communion with our Maker. It is an effort not of the intellect but of the heart. Communion with God may come soon or it may take years or even ages. It is enough if the effort is sincere and heart-felt.

—Vol. 68, November 7, 1938

PRAYER PURIFIES THE HEART

I have not the slightest doubt that prayer is an unfailing means of cleansing the heart of passions. But it must be combined with the utmost humility.

—*The Story of My Experiments with Truth,* Vol. 39

Prayer is for remembering God and for purifying the heart and can be offered even when observing silence.

—*Selected Works,* Vol. 6, April 20, 1947, 120

We may miss many things in life but not prayer, which implies our cooperation with God and with one another. Prayer should be a bath of purification for the spirit of humanity. Physical health suffers if we do not wash our bodies; similarly the spirit becomes unclean if the heart is not washed with prayer. Please therefore never be negligent in prayer.

—*Selected Works,* Vol. 5, December 31, 1926, 373

•

Prayer is not to be performed with the lips, but with the heart. And that is why it can be performed equally by the dumb and the stammerer, by the ignorant and the stupid. And the prayers of those whose tongues are nectared but whose hearts are full of poison are never heard. Those who would pray to God must cleanse their hearts. It is faith that steers us through stormy seas, faith that moves mountains, and faith that jumps across the ocean. That faith is nothing but a living, wide-awake consciousness of God within. The one who has achieved that faith wants nothing. Bodily diseased he is spiritually healthy, physically pure, he rolls in spiritual riches.

The language of the lips is easily taught; but who can teach the language of the heart? Only the true devotee knows it and can teach it. I have therefore suggested the religion of service as the means. God seeks for God's seat the heart of the one who serves humanity. A prayerful heart is the vehicle and service makes the heart prayerful. —Vol. 28, September 24, 1925

THE HUMILITY OF PRAYER

One cannot pray to God for help in a spirit of pride, but only if one confesses oneself as helpless. As I lie in bed, every day I realize how insignificant we are, how very full of attachments and aversions, and what evil desires sway us. Often I am filled with shame by unworthiness of my mind. Many a time I fall into despair because of the attention my body craves and wish that it should perish. From my condition, I can very well judge that of others.   —Vol. 15, November 26, 1918

If you would ask God to help you, you would go to God in all your nakedness, approach God without reservations, also without fear or doubts as to how God can help a fallen being like you. God, who has helped millions who have approached him, is God going to desert you? God makes no exceptions whatsoever, and you will find that every one of your prayers will be answered. The prayer of even the more impure will be answered. I am telling this out of my personal experience. I have gone through the purgatory. Seek first the Kingdom of Heaven, and everything will be added unto you.   —Vol. 40, April 4, 1929

•

God is within everyone. Nothing happens without God's permission. Our prayer is a heart search. It is a reminder to ourselves that we are helpless without God's support. No effort is complete without prayer, with a definite recognition that the best human endeavor is of no effect if it does not have God's blessings behind it. Prayer is a call to humility. It is a call to self-purification, to inward search.   —Vol. 61, June 8, 1935

THE PRACTICE OF PRAYER

There are at least two clear times for prayer. We should turn our mind to the Lord immediately upon awakening in the morning and when closing our eyes for sleep in the evening. During the rest of the day, every man and woman who is spiritually awake will think of God when doing anything and do that with God as witness. Such persons will never do anything evil, and a time will come when they will think every thought with God as witness and as its Master. This will be a state in which such persons will have reduced themselves to ciphers. Such persons, who live constantly in the sight of God, will every moment feel God dwelling in their hearts.

We have only to turn our thoughts to God, no matter by what name we call God, by what method and in what condition. Very few form such a habit. If most people followed this practice, there would be less sin and evil in this world and our dealings with one another would be pure. In order that we may attain such a pure state, we should pray at least at the two times which I have mentioned. We may fix other hours, too, according to our convenience, and gradually increase their frequency so that ultimately our every breath will be accompanied with the name of God.

Such individual prayer consumes no time at all. It requires not time but wakefulness. As we do not feel that the unceasing action of blinking consumes any time, so also we do not feel that praying inwardly does. But we are aware that the eyelids are doing their work; similarly prayer should go on constantly in our heart. Those who wish to pray in this manner should know that they cannot do so with an impure heart. They must, therefore, banish all impurity from their heart when praying. As one feels ashamed of doing anything wicked when being observed by somebody, so also should one feel ashamed of acting similarly in the sight of God. But God watches our every action and every thought. There is not a single moment when we can think any thought or do any act unknown to God. Those who thus pray from the bottom of their heart will in time be filled with the spirit of God and become sinless. — Vol. 50, July 17, 1932

•

I agree that, if a person could practice the presence of God all the twenty-four hours there would be no need for a separate time for prayer. But most people find this impossible. The sordid everyday world is too much with them. For them the practice of complete withdrawal of the mind from all outward things, even though it might be only for a few minutes every day, will be found to be of infinite help. Silent communion will help them to experience an undisturbed peace in the midst of turmoil to curb anger and cultivate patience.

—*Selected Works,* Vol. 6, April 28, 1946, 121

•

Prayer is the key of the morning and the bolt of the evening.

—*Selected Works,* Vol. 6, January 23, 1930, 121

•

Prayer is the first and the last lesson in learning the noble and brave art of sacrificing self in the various walks of life culminating in the defense of one's nation's liberty and honor. Undoubtedly, prayer requires a living faith in God.

—*Selected Works,* Vol. 6, April 14, 1946, 116–17

•

True meditation consists in closing the eyes and ears of the mind to all else except the object of one's devotion. Hence the closing eyes during prayer is an aid to such concentration. Humanity's conception of God is naturally limited. Each one has, therefore, to think of God as best appeals, provided that the conception is pure and uplifting.   —Vol. 85, August 18, 1946

PRAYER IS NEVER FRUITLESS

A prayer can be offered in connection with some person or thing, and may even be granted. But if it is offered without any such specific end in view, it will confer a greater benefit on the world as well as ourselves. Prayer exerts an influence over us; our soul becomes more vigilant, and the greater its vigilance, the wider the sphere of its influence. Prayer is a function of the heart. We speak aloud in order to wake it up. The Power that pervades the universe is also present in the human heart. The body does not offer it any obstruction. The obstruction is something of our own making and is removed by prayer. We can never know if a prayer has or has not yielded the desired result. Prayer is never fruitless, but we cannot know the fruit of it. Nor should we imagine that it is a good thing if it yields the desired result. Here too the Bhagavad Gita doctrine has to be practiced. We may pray for something and yet remain free from attachment. We may pray for the salvation of others but should not worry whether they get or do not get what we want for them. Even if the result is just the opposite of what we had asked for, that is no reason for the conclusion that the prayer has been fruitless.

—*Selected Works,* Vol. 5, July 17, 1932, 381

•

I am certain that prayer does us a world of good. You will realize its value in times of trouble and even from day to day if you offer it thoughtfully. Prayer is food for the soul. As the body languishes for want of nourishment, even so does the soul wither away without her appropriate food.

—*Selected Works,* Vol. 5, June 2, 1919, 381

•

God answers prayer in God's own way, not ours. God's ways are different from the ways of mortals. Hence they are inscrutable. Prayer presupposes faith. No prayer goes in vain. Prayer is like any other action. It bears fruit whether we see it or not, and the fruit of the heart, prayer, is far more potent than so-called action.

—*Selected Works,* Vol. 6, June 29, 1947, 122–23

MY EXPERIENCE OF PRAYER

Prayer has saved my life. Without it, I should have been a lunatic long ago. I had my share of the bitterest public and private experiences. They threw me into temporary despair. If I was able to get rid of that despair, it was because of prayer. It has not been a part of my life as truth has been. It came out of sheer necessity, as I found myself in a plight where I could not possibly be happy without it. And as time went on, my faith in God increased, and more irresistible became the yearning for prayer. Life seemed to be dull and vacant without it. I had attended the Christian service in South Africa, but it had failed to grip me. I could not join them in it. They supplicated God, I could not. I started with disbelief in God and prayer, and until at a late stage in life, I did not feel anything like a void in life. But at that stage, I felt that as food is indispensable for the body, so was prayer indispensable for the soul. In fact food for the body is not so necessary as prayer for the soul. For starvation is often necessary to keep the body in health, but there is no such thing as prayer starvation. You cannot possibly have a surfeit of prayer. Three of the greatest teachers of the world — Buddha, Jesus, and Mohammed — have left unimpeachable testimony that they found illumination through prayer and could not possibly live without it. Millions of Hindus, Muslims, and Christians find their only solace in life in prayer. Either you call them liars or self-deluded people.

—Vol. 47, September 5, 1931

When I pray, I do not ask for anything, but I simply think of some of the verses from scripture or hymns which I fancy for the moment. The relation between God and myself is, not only at prayer but at all times, that of master and slave in perpetual bondage. Prayer is to me the intense longing of the heart to merge myself in the Maker. If we do not pray, evidently we have no longing; there is no feeling of helplessness and when there is no helplessness, there is no need for help.   —Vol. 31, October 30, 1926

A NATIONAL DAY
OF PRAYER AND FASTING

Prayer expresses the soul's longing and fasting sets the soul free for efficacious prayer. In my opinion, a national fast and day of national prayer should be accompanied by the suspension of business. I therefore without hesitation advise suspension of business provided it is carried out with calmness and dignity and provided it is entirely voluntary. Those who are required for necessary work such as hospital, sanitation, off-loading of steamers, etc.

should not be entitled to suspend work. And I suggest that on this day of fasting there are no processions and no meetings. People should remain indoors and devote themselves entirely to prayer.

I would urge the modern generation not to regard fasting and prayer with skepticism or distrust. The greatest teachers of the world have derived extraordinary powers for the good of humanity and attained clarity of vision through fasting and prayer. Much of this discipline runs to waste because instead of being a matter of the heart, it is often resorted to for stage effect. I would therefore warn the bodies of this movement against any such maneuvering. Let them have a living faith in what they urge or let them drop it. Whether Hindus or Muslims, we have all got the religious spirit in us. Let us not be undermined by our playing at religion. — Vol. 16, October 4, 1919

THE METHOD OF FASTING

Fasting for the sake of unfoldment of the spirit is a discipline I hold to be absolutely necessary at some stage or other in the evolution of an individual. Crucifixion of the flesh is a meaningless term unless one goes voluntarily through pangs of hunger. For one thing, identification with the starving poor is a meaningless term without the experience behind it.

— *Selected Works*, Vol. 5, August 29, 1926, 402–3

Fasting should be inspired by perfect truth and perfect non-violence. The call for it should come from within and it should not be imitative. It should never be undertaken for a selfish purpose, but for the benefit of others only. A fast is out of the question in a case where there is hatred for anybody. But what is the inner voice? Is every one capable of hearing it? These are big questions. The inner voice is there in every one of us, but one whose ears are not open for it cannot hear it, just as a deaf person is unable to hear the sweetest of songs. Self-restraint is essential in order to make our ears fit to hear the voice of God.

— *Selected Works*, Vol. 5, October 30, 1932, 403

There can be no room for selfishness, anger, lack of faith, or impatience in a pure fast. Infinite patience, firm resolve, single-mindedness of purpose, perfect calm, and no anger must of necessity be there. But since it is impossible for us to develop all these qualities all at once, those who have not devoted themselves to following the laws of nonviolence should undertake a satyagrahi fast.   —*Selected Works,* Vol. 6, October 13, 1940, 216

A DAILY RESOLUTION

Let our first act every morning be to make the following resolve for the day: "I shall not fear anyone on earth. I shall fear only God; I shall not bear ill will toward anyone. I shall not submit to injustice from anyone. I shall conquer untruth by truth and in resisting untruth I shall put up with all suffering."   —Vol. 15, May 4, 1919

GANDHI'S PRAYER

Lord of humility, dwelling in the little pariah hut, help us to search for Thee. Give us receptiveness, give us open-heartedness, give us your humility. Give us the ability and willingness to identify ourselves with the masses of India.

O God, who does help only when humanity feels utterly humble, grant that we may not be isolated from the people we would serve as servants and friends. Let us be embodiments of self-sacrifice, embodiments of Godliness, humility personified, that we may know the land better and love it more.

—Vol. 58, September 12, 1934; the only prayer
composed by Gandhi recorded in all his *Collected Works*

THE WEAPON OF PRAYER

I have no strength save what God gives me. I have no authority over my compatriots save the purely moral. If God holds me to

be a pure instrument for the spread of nonviolence in the place of the awful violence now ruling the earth, God will give me the strength and show me the way. My greatest weapon is mute prayer. The cause of peace is, therefore, in God's good hands. Nothing can happen but by God's will expressed in God's eternal, changeless Law which is God. We neither know God nor God's Law save through the glass darkly. But the faint glimpse of the Law is sufficient to fill me with joy, hope, and faith in the future.
— Vol. 71, December 5, 1939

LEAVE THE RESULTS IN GOD'S HANDS

You must not worry whether the desired result follows from your action or not, so long as your motive is pure, your means correct. Really, it means that things will come right in the end if you take care of the means and leave the rest to God.
— Vol. 84, April 7, 1946

Success or failure is not in our hands. It is enough if we do our part well. Ours is but to strive. In the end, it will be as God wishes.   — *Selected Works,* Vol. 6, January 12, 1947, 152

LIVE A SAINTLY LIFE TO OBTAIN PEACE

Only by living a saintly life can one obtain peace. This is the way to fulfillment in this world and the next. A saintly life is that in which we practice truth, nonviolence, and restraint. Enjoyment of pleasures can never be one's dharma. Dharma has its source in renunciation only.

It is possible to atone for one's past misdeeds, and it is our duty to do so. Atonement is not supplication, nor crying or whimpering, though there is some scope for fasting. Repentance is the true atonement. In other words, the resolve not to commit the mistake again is without doubt the true repentance. The results of the misdeeds are wiped out to some extent. Until we atone for a sin, it goes on accumulating like compound interest. This stops once we do the penance.

The aim of humanity in this life is self-realization. The one and only means of attaining this is to spend one's life in serving humanity in a true altruistic spirit and to lose oneself in this and to realize the oneness of life.   —Vol. 41, August 15, 1929

GOD GIVES ENOUGH LIGHT
FOR THE NEXT STEP

When we know that God is the mystery of mysteries, why should anything that God does perplex us? If God acted as we would have God do or if God acted exactly like us, we would not be God's creatures and God our Creator. The impenetrable darkness that surrounds us is not a curse but a blessing. God has given us power to see the steps in front of us, and it would be enough if Heavenly Light reveals that step to us. We can then sing with Cardinal Newman, "Lead Kindly Light. One step enough for me." And we may be sure from our past experience that the next step will always be in view. In other words, the impenetrable darkness is nothing so impenetrable as we may imagine. But it seems impenetrable when in our impatience we want to look beyond that one step. And since God is love, we can say definitely that even the physical catastrophes that God sends now and then must be a blessing in disguise and they can be so only to those who regard them as a warning for introspection and self-purification.

—*Selected Works*, Vol. 5, March 31, 1934, 355

6

The Urgent Need
for Nuclear Disarmament

"I did not move a muscle when I first heard that the atom bomb had wiped out Hiroshima," Gandhi told an interviewer. "On the contrary, I said to myself, 'Unless now the world adopts nonviolence, it will spell certain suicide for humanity.' Nonviolence is the only thing the atom bomb cannot destroy."

Gandhi rooted his political work for independence in his faith in God and God's way of nonviolence. During the early 1940s, he publicly opposed World War II and was imprisoned for speaking out against war. From the moment he heard about the U.S. atomic bombings of Hiroshima on August 6, 1945, and Nagasaki on August 9, 1945, until a few hours before his assassination on January 30, 1948, Gandhi condemned nuclear weapons and urged the world, especially the United States, to stop developing, maintaining, and preparing to use them. At the time of their use, Gandhi was recognized as the greatest spiritual leader in the world and became the greatest critic of nuclear weapons. Any survey of his message must include his spiritual reflections on the use of nuclear weapons.

Gandhi's stand against nuclear weapons was integral to his faith in God. Indeed in one of his most important statements, cited below, he commented on the spiritual consequences of building and maintaining nuclear weapons. Gandhi astutely observed that it was clear what nuclear weapons had physically done to Japan, but that it would take some time before it became apparent what the use of nuclear weapons had done spiritually to the soul of the people of the United States.

Gandhi spoke of nuclear weapons in religious terms. Like Dorothy Day, he named the development and use of them as a mortal sin. "I regard the employment of the atom bomb for the wholesale destruction of men, women, and children as the most diabolical use of science," Gandhi said. "The atom bomb is the weapon of ultimate brute force and destruction. The atom bomb mentality is immoral, unethical, addictive, and only evil can come of it."

Today, the United States maintains over thirty thousand nuclear weapons with no international movement toward disarmament. In 1998, India exploded three nuclear weapons at Pokhran, and Pakistan followed with explosions of its own a few days later. Even after the collapse of communism and the end of the Cold War, the world continues to hang on the brink of nuclear destruction. Gandhi's appeal for nuclear disarmament remains as critical as ever.

"The country that adopts a policy of total disarmament, without waiting for its neighbors, will be able to lead the world away from hatred, fear, and mistrust toward the true community, the harmony of all people."

"Even if I am alone," Gandhi wrote to Lord Mountbatten, the last British viceroy, "I swear by nonviolence and truth together standing for the highest order of courage, before which the atom bomb pales into insignificance."

NONVIOLENCE AND NUCLEAR WEAPONS

Nonviolence is the only antidote against the atom bomb. Truth and nonviolence are more powerful than the atom bomb.

A nation or a group which has made nonviolence its final policy cannot be subjected to slavery even by the atom bomb.

—Vol. 85, August 8, 1946

My faith in nonviolence and truth is being strengthened all the more in spite of the increasing number of atom bombs. I have not a shadow of a doubt that there is no power superior to the power of truth and nonviolence in the world. See what a great difference there is between the two: one is moral and spiritual force and is motivated by infinite soul-force; the other is a product of physical and artificial power, which is perishable.

—Vol. 87, April 17, 1947

•

I hold that those who invented the atom bomb have committed the gravest sin in the world of science. The only weapon that can save the world is nonviolence. Considering the trend of the world, I might appear a fool to everyone. But I do not feel sorry for it. I rather consider it a great blessing that God did not make me capable of inventing the atom bomb.

—Vol. 87, April 25, 1947

•

Look at Japan, look at Germany. The very violence which brought them to the pinnacle of power has razed them to the ground. And has not the atom bomb proved the futility of all violence? And yet we are crazy enough to think that we can win independence by breaking a few skulls. I am sure, out of this orgy of violence, people will learn the lesson of nonviolence.

—Vol. 83, March 3, 1946

So far as I can see, the atomic bomb has deadened the finest feeling that has sustained humanity for ages. There used to be the so-called laws of war, which made it tolerable. Now we know the naked truth. War knows no law except that of might.

The atom bomb brought an empty victory to the Allied arms, but it resulted for the time being in destroying Japan. What has happened to the soul of the destroying nation is yet too early to see.

Forces of nature act in a mysterious manner. We can but solve the mystery by deducing the unknown result from the known

results of similar events. Slaveholders cannot hold slaves without putting themselves or their deputy in the cage holding the
slave. Let no one run away with the idea that I wish to put in
a defense of Japan's misdeeds in pursuance of Japan's unworthy
ambition. The difference was only one of degree. I assume that
Japan's greed was more unworthy. But the greater unworthiness
conferred no right on the less unworthy of destroying without
mercy men, women, and children of Japan in a particular area.

The moral to be legitimately drawn from the supreme tragedy
of the bomb is that it will not be destroyed by counter-bombs,
even as violence cannot be by counter-violence. Humanity has to
get out of violence only through nonviolence. Hatred can be overcome only by love. Counter-hatred only increases the surface as
well as the depth of hatred.   —Vol. 84, July 1, 1946

•

Violence can only be effectively met by nonviolence. This is an
old established truth, that the weapon of violence, even if it was
the atom bomb, became useless when matched against true nonviolence. That very few understand how to wield this weapon is
true. It requires a lot of understanding and strength of mind. It
is unlike what is needed in military schools and colleges. What
it requires is purity of the mind. The difficulty one experiences
in meeting violence with nonviolence arises from weakness of
the mind.   —Vol. 88, May 25, 1947

In this age of the atom bomb, unadulterated nonviolence is
the only force that can confound all the tricks put together of
violence.   —Vol. 89, November 16, 1947

Violence can only be overcome through nonviolence. This is as
clear to me as the proposition that two and two make four. But
for this one must have faith. Even a weapon like the atom bomb
when used against nonviolence will prove ineffective. This applies
to true nonviolence. Faith by itself also will not do. It must be
supplemented by knowledge. Training in nonviolence is not to be

had like training in the use of weapons in military training. It requires purity of heart and soul-force.

—Vol. 90, December 3, 1947

Nonviolence is soul force and the soul is imperishable, changeless, and eternal. The atom bomb is the acme of physical force and, as such, subject to the law of dissipation, decay, and death that governs the physical universe. Our scriptures bear witness that when soul-force is fully awakened in us, it becomes irresistible. But the test and condition of full awakening is that it must permeate every pore of our being and emanate with every breath that we breathe.   —*All Men Are Brothers,* 90

DISARM NOW
OR THERE IS NO HOPE FOR PEACE

I have no doubt that unless big nations shed their desire for exploitation and the spirit of violence of which war is the natural expression and the atom bomb the inevitable consequence, there is no hope for peace in the world.   —Vol. 86, November 10, 1946

The world has reached the stage of atomic warfare in returning violence for violence. Let us pray to God that God may save us from this atom bomb mentality. Peace through superior violence inevitably led to the atom bomb and all that it stood for. It was the complete negation of nonviolence and of democracy which was not possible without the former. The nonviolent resistance now required demands a courage of a superior order to that needed in violent warfare.   —Vol. 87, March 11, 1947

GANDHI'S LAST WORDS

On January 30, 1948, just a few hours before Gandhi was assassinated, LIFE *magazine journalist Margaret Bourke-White asked him about the atom bomb. "Would you advise America to give up the manufacture of atom bombs?" she asked. Gandhi replied:*

Most certainly. As things are, the war has ended disastrously and the victors are vanquished by jealousy and lust for power. Already a third war is being canvassed. Nonviolence is a mightier weapon by far than the atom bomb. Even if the people of Hiroshima could have died in their thousands with prayer and goodwill in their hearts, the situation would have been transformed, as if by a miracle.

"How would you meet the atom bomb with nonviolence?" Margaret Bourke-White asked. Gandhi answered:

I will not go underground. I will not go into shelter. I will come out in the open and let the pilot see that I have not a trace of ill will against him. The pilot will not see our faces from his great height, I know. But the longing in our hearts that he will not come to harm would reach up to him and his eyes would be opened. If those thousands who were done to death in Hiroshima, if they had died with that prayerful action — died openly with that prayer in their hearts — their sacrifice would not have gone in vain.   — Vol. 90, January 30, 1948

7

The Life of Steadfast Resistance

For over fifty years, Mahatma Gandhi issued thousands of statements, press releases, messages, and leaflets against racism, imperialism, injustice, and war and in support of equality, independence, justice, and peace. Meanwhile, he wrote tens of thousands of letters, nearly all by hand with a short pencil stub. He spent a good deal of his time every single day for over fifty years writing, trying to proclaim the truth as he saw it, in whatever way he could.

Gandhi was convinced that the spiritual life required daily engagement with the world, with the poor, with one's enemies, with every person one met. Throughout his life, he shared his faith in God and nonviolence and steadfastly resisted the forces of evil. Long before the age of television, computers, and the Internet, Gandhi communicated his message as widely as possible. As his statements and letters reveal, Gandhi was immensely determined, profoundly disciplined, and always hopeful that others would embrace his passion for truth and nonviolence. He remained compassionate toward his opponents, inspiring to his followers, and affectionate toward his friends. Besides the hundreds of millions who adored him, Gandhi was greatly loved, of course, by his wife, his adopted British daughter, Mirabehn, and his relatives, community members, movement colleagues, and friends, who wrote him weekly for decades. Two lifelong friends, Charlie Andrews, a Christian minister, and Hermann Kallenbach, a Jewish philanthropist, corresponded regularly. In 1990, over five hundred long, hand-written letters by Gandhi to Kallenbach were discovered in South Africa, revealing new insights not only into Gandhi's search for God and the satyagraha struggle, but an astonishing devotion to friendship.

This chapter includes selections from some of Gandhi's most famous speeches, statements, and letters.

VICTORY IS OURS
The Johannesburg, South Africa, Mass Meeting, September 11, 1906

In 1906, the white South African government proposed tightening its racist oppression against the Indian commu-nity by requiring all Indians to be fingerprinted and to carry registration cards. Gandhi's impromptu speech before three thousand Indians living in South Africa on September 11, 1906, inspired them to vow to disobey the racist laws in a spirit of nonviolence, "come what may," and marked the beginning of the Satyagraha movement.

We all believe in one and the same God, the differences of nomenclature in Hinduism and Islam notwithstanding. To pledge ourselves or to take an oath in the name of that God or with God as witness is not something to be trifled with. If having taken such an oath we violate our pledge, we are guilty before God and humanity. Personally, I hold that those who deliberately and intelligently take a pledge and then break it forfeit their humanity.

Sheth Haji Habib is proposing to administer an oath of such a serious character. There is no one in this meeting who can be classed as an infant or as wanting in understanding. You are all well advanced in age and have seen the world. Many of you are delegates and have discharged responsibilities in a greater or lesser measure. None of us present, therefore, can ever hope to excuse ourselves by saying that we did not know what we were about when we took the oath.

I know that pledges and vows are, and should be, taken on rare occasions. A person who takes a vow every now and then is sure to stumble. But if I can imagine a crisis in the history of the Indian community of South Africa when it would be in the fitness of things to take pledges, that crisis is surely now. There is wisdom in taking serious steps with great caution and hesitation. But caution and hesitation have their limits, which we have now passed. The government has taken leave of all sense of decency. We would only be betraying our unworthiness and cowardice, if we cannot stake our all in the face of the conflagration which envelopes us and sit watching it with folded hands. There is no doubt, therefore, that the present is a proper occasion for taking pledges.

But every one of us must think out for ourselves if we have the will and the ability to pledge ourselves. Resolutions of this nature cannot be passed by a majority vote. Only those who take a pledge can be bound by it. This pledge must not be taken with a view to produce an effect on outsiders. No one should trouble to consider what impression it might have upon the local government, the imperial government, or the government of India. We must search only our own hearts, and if the inner voice assures us that we have the requisite strength to carry us through, then only should we pledge ourselves and then only would our pledge bear fruit.

A few words now as to the consequences. Hoping for the best, we may say that, if a majority of the Indians pledge themselves to resistance and if all who take the pledge prove true to themselves, the Ordinance may not even be passed and, if passed, may be soon repealed. It may be that we may not be called upon to suffer at all.

But if on the one hand, those who take a pledge must be robust optimists, on the other hand, they must be prepared for the worst. It is therefore that I would give you an idea of the worst that might happen to us in the present struggle. Imagine that all of us present here numbering three thousand at the most pledge ourselves. Imagine again that the remaining ten thousand Indians [in South Africa] take no such pledge. We will only provoke ridicule in the beginning. Again, it is quite possible that in spite of the present warning some or many of those who pledge themselves might weaken at the very first trial. We might have to go to jail, where we might be insulted. We might have to go hungry and suffer extreme heat or cold. Hard labor might be imposed on us. We might be flogged by rude warders. We might be fined heavily and our property might be attacked and held up to auction if there are only a few resisters left. Opulent today, we might be reduced to abject poverty tomorrow. We might be deported. Suffering from starvation and similar hardships in jail, some of us might fall ill and even die.

In short, therefore, it is not at all impossible that we might have to endure every hardship that we can imagine, and wisdom lies in pledging ourselves on the understanding that we shall have to suffer all that and worse. If someone asks me when and how the struggle may end, I may say that, if the entire community humanly stands the tests, the end will be near. If many of us fall back under storm and stress, the struggle will be prolonged.

But I can boldly declare, and with certainty, that so long as there is even a handful of people true to their pledge, there can only be one end to the struggle, and that is victory.

— Vol. 5, September 11, 1906

OBEYING THE DIVINE LAW, RESISTING UNJUST LAWS

The time to test the strength of the obnoxious law is approaching. All Indians [in South Africa] will be anxiously watching what the government does on August 1st [1907]. To speak the truth, however, we should wait with courage, not with anxiety. Any pain we suffer in order to save ourselves from the obnoxious law must be counted as pleasure. Every Indian should pray, "Let me be the first to go to jail, so that my sisters and brothers are spared the pain."

We have already examined the various reasons why we ought not to submit to the obnoxious law. It should be noted that in defying this murderous law, we obey the divine law. To submit to the unjust law will be a sin. Likewise, it will be a sin to violate the divine law. The one who abides by the divine law will win bliss in this world, as also in the next. What is this divine law? It is that one has to suffer pain before enjoying pleasure and that one's true self-interest consists in the good of all, which means that we should suffer and die for others.

When a lump of earth is broken into dust, it mixes with water and nourishes plant life. It is by sacrificing themselves that plants sustain every kind of animal life. Animals sacrifice themselves for the good of their progeny. The mother suffers unbearable pain at the time of childbirth, but feels only happy in that suffering. Both the mother and the father undergo hardships in bringing up their children. Wherever communities and nations exist, individual members of those communities or nations have endured hardships for the common good.

In the sixth century B.C., after wandering from forest to forest, braving the extremes of heat and cold and suffering many privations, Buddha attained self-realization and spread ideas of spiritual welfare among the people. Nineteen hundred years ago, Jesus Christ, according to the Christian belief, dedicated his life to the people and suffered many insults and hardships. The prophet Mohammed suffered much. People had prepared themselves for an attack on his life. He paid no heed to it. These great and holy ones obeyed the law stated above and brought happiness to humanity. They did not think of their personal interest but found their own happiness in the happiness of others.

One must pass through suffering before tasting happiness. For public good, men and women have to suffer hardships even to the point of death. Let us go further. It is a sin to violate one's pledge — to betray humanity with which we are endowed.

Today it has fallen to the lot of the Indian community in the Transvaal in South Africa to submit to this great divine law. So persuaded, we congratulate our compatriots . They have the opportunity now to see the Indian community throughout South Africa gaining its freedom through them. How could such great happiness come to us without our going through equally great suffering?

Our petition is no longer addressed to humanity, but to God. Day and night, God listens to our pleas, our petitions. God hears the petitions of all at the same time. With the purest heart therefore we pray to God that our brothers and sisters in the Transvaal may be prepared to suffer fearlessly anything that may befall them in August, placing their trust in God alone, and with only God's name on their lips.   —Vol. 7, July 27, 1907

GOD WILL GIVE US OUR RIGHTS
Speech upon Release from Prison, Johannesburg, South Africa

I see you today after two months and ten days in jail. I felt as if I was outside all the time and not in jail. It is today that I think I have entered a prison. Those who are outside have a more important duty to discharge than those in jail. So long as people who are outside do not exert themselves more vigorously, our bonds are not likely to snap. When the station-master at the Volksrust jail congratulated me on my release, I told him also that it was really on that day that I found myself in prison, and that I was now facing much heavier tasks than those assigned to me while in jail.

In a country where people suffer injustice and oppression and are denied their legitimate rights, their real duty lies in suffering imprisonment. And further, so long as the bonds that bind us have not been snapped, I think it is better that we spend our days in jail. This, I think, is the true meaning of religion for those who have faith in God.

I want to say a few words about the scene that was witnessed at the station today. My services have pleased the community. You have assembled today in such a large number because you wish to express your appreciation of my having worked [in jail] at breaking stones, of my having suffered imprisonment, and of the other things that I did.

Where there is God, there is truth, and where there is truth, there is God. I live in fear of God. I love truth only, and so God is with me. Even if the path of truth does not please the community, it pleases God. Therefore I will do what pleases God, even if the community should turn against me. The enthusiasm that was in evidence today was heartening. It shows that all of you, like others who could not be present, approve of the satyagraha campaign that we have launched.

I have said at other places that the outcome of our campaign does not depend upon whether we win or lose in the Supreme Court. We should rather, if need be, bear separation from our families, sacrifice our property for the sake of truth, endure whatever other hardships we may encounter, and thus make the voice of truth heard in the Divine Court. When the echoes of that voice strike the ears of General Smuts [the prime minister of Transvaal, South Africa], his conscience will be stirred and he will acknowledge our rights, will see that we invite suffering in order to secure them, and that we have suffered more than enough. It is then that we shall get what we have been demanding.

It is not the imperial government that will secure you your rights. You will get them only from God. If you fight truthfully with God as witness, your bonds will be loosened. God is present everywhere. God sees and hears everything. I am sure that we shall be free when God stirs our opponents' conscience. We do not sacrifice as much as we should. But the moment we do so, our fetters will fall away.   —Vol. 9, December 12, 1908

TO SERVE WITH ONE'S WHOLE LIFE
The Draft Constitution for the Satyagraha Ashram, Ahmedabad, India

The Constitution for the Ashram was revised throughout Gandhi's life and the subject of many speeches and articles. It outlined the religious vows and core principles of ashram life.

The object of the Ashram is to learn how to serve India with one's whole life and [then] to serve it, not inconsistent with universal welfare. In order to learn how to serve the country, the following observances should be enforced on one's life.

1. The Vow of Truth

It is not enough for persons under this vow that they do not ordinarily resort to untruth. Such persons ought to know that no deception may be practiced even for the good of the country.

2. The Vow of Nonviolence

It is not enough to refrain from taking the life of any living being. Those who have pledged to this vow may not kill even those whom they believe to be unjust. They may not be angry with them. They must love them. Thus, they would oppose the tyranny whether of parents, governments, or others, but will never kill or hurt the tyrant. The followers of truth and nonviolence will offer satyagraha against tyranny and win over the tyrant by love. They will not carry out the tyrant's will but will suffer punishment even unto death for disobeying the tyrant's will until the tyrant himself is won over.

3. The Vow of Celibacy

It is well-nigh impossible to observe these two vows unless celibacy too is observed. And for this vow, it is not enough that one does not look upon another with a lustful eye. One has so to control the animal passions that they will not be moved even in thought. If one is married, one will not have sexual intercourse even with one's spouse, but will regard the spouse as a friend and establish a relationship of perfect purity.

4. The Vow of Control of the Palate

Until one has overcome the palate, it is difficult to observe the foregoing vows, more especially that of celibacy. Control of the palate should therefore be treated as a separate observance by those desirous of serving the country and, believing that eating is only for sustaining the body, they should regulate and purify their diet day by day. Such persons will immediately or gradually as they can leave off such articles of food as may tend to stimulate animal passions.

5. The Vow of Nonstealing

It is not enough not to steal what is commonly considered as another's property. One who has pledged this vow should realize that Nature provides from day to day just enough and no more for one's daily need by way of food and so hold it as theft to use articles of food and clothing which one does not really need and live accordingly.

6. The Vow of Nonpossession

It is not enough not to possess and keep much, but it is necessary not to keep anything which may not be absolutely necessary for the nourishment and protection of our body. Thus, if one can do without chairs, one should do so. Those who have taken this vow will always bear this in mind and endeavor to simplify their life more and more.

7. The Vow of Swadeshi

The person who has taken the vow of Swadeshi will never use articles, such as foreign clothing, which conceivably involve violation of truth in their manufacture or on the part of their manufacturers. It follows, for instance, that a votary of truth will not use articles manufactured in the mills of England, Germany, or India, for we cannot be sure that they involve no such violation of truth. Moreover, laborers suffer much in the mills. The generation of tremendous heat causes enormous destruction of life. Foreign cloth and cloth made by means of machinery are therefore tabooed to a votary of nonviolence as they involve triple violence. Further reflection will show that the use of foreign cloth can be held to involve a break of the vows of nonstealing and nonpossession. Therefore the vow of Swadeshi requires the use of simple clothing made on simple handlooms and stitched in simple style avoiding foreign buttons, etc. The same line of reasoning may be applied to all other articles.

8. The Vow of Fearlessness

The one who is acted upon by fear can hardly observe the vows of truth and nonviolence. [Those who profess this vow] will

therefore constantly endeavor to be free from the fear of kings or
society, from one's caste or family, from thieves or robbers, from
ferocious animals such as tigers, and even of death. Those who
observe the vow of fearlessness will defend themselves or others
by truth-force or soul-force.

9. The Vow of Removal of Untouchability

Untouchability, which has deep roots in Hinduism, is altogether
irreligious. The so-called untouchables have an equal place in the
ashram. The ashram does not believe in caste, which it considers
has injured Hinduism, because its implications of superior and
inferior status, and of pollution by contact, are contrary to the
law of love.

10. The Vow of Tolerance

The ashram believes that the principal faiths of the world constitute a revelation of Truth, but as they have all been outlined by
imperfect people, they have been affected by imperfections and
alloyed with untruth. One must therefore entertain the same respect for the religious faith of others as for one's own. Where
such tolerance becomes a law of life, conflict between different
faiths becomes impossible, and so does all effort to convert others
to one's own faith. One can only pray that the defects in the various faiths may be overcome, and that they advance, side by side,
toward perfection.   —Vol. 13, May 20, 1915;
                        later a vow of physical labor was added;
            see also, in particular, the 1928 revised Constitution

THE HINDU MISSION OF NONVIOLENCE

Truth and nonviolence are our goal. Nonviolence is the supreme
dharma. There is no discovery of greater import than this. So
long as we engage in mundane actions, so long as soul and body
are together, some violence will continue to occur through our
agency. But we must renounce at least the violence that it is
possible for us to renounce. We should understand that the less

violence a religion permits, the more is the truth contained in it. If we can ensure the deliverance of India, it is only through truth and nonviolence.

Love is a rare herb that makes a friend even of a sworn enemy, and this herb grows out of nonviolence. What in a dormant state is nonviolence becomes love in the waking state. Love destroys ill will. We should love all, whether the English or the Muslims. We should act only through love. Thus alone shall we succeed. So long as we do not have unshakable faith in truth, love, and nonviolence, we can make no progress. If we give up these and imitate European civilization, we shall be doomed.

Be fearless. So long as you live under various kinds of fears, you can never progress, you can never succeed. Never, never give up truth and love. Treat all enemies and friends with love.

— Vol. 14, speech to a Hindu conference, March 30, 1918

LOVE EVER DIES
Satyagraha Leaflet Number 20,
For the National Strike

My one request to Hindus, Muslims, Parsis, Christians, and Jews is that by our conduct tomorrow we may demonstrate to the government our absolutely harmless intentions and show that nobody wishes to commit a breach of the peace, and further show that we are capable of discharging heavy responsibilities with patient calmness. We should at the same time demonstrate that we are capable of acting in perfect unity and determined to secure a fulfillment of our cherished will. But we do not desire to obtain justice by harboring ill will against the government but by goodwill.

Hatred ever kills. Love ever dies. Such is the vast difference between the two. What is obtained by love is retained for all time. What is obtained by hatred, proves a burden in reality, for it increases hatred. The duty of human beings is to diminish hatred and to promote love. I pray that all will observe the full hartal and fast and pray and do all this in a loving spirit.

— Vol. 15, May 10, 1919, on the eve of the national strike

THE GREAT TRIAL
Statement to the Judge, 1922

Gandhi was allowed to make a statement in court be-
fore sentencing on March 18, 1922, after the British had
arrested him for sedition. Gandhi's speech electrified the na-
tion. After Gandhi spoke, the British judge sentenced him to
six years in prison. No British judge ever invited Gandhi to
make a statement in court again.

Nonviolence is the first article of my faith. It is also the last article of my creed. But I had to make my choice. I had either
to submit to a system which I had considered had done an ir-
reparable harm to my country, or incur the risk of the mad fury
of my people bursting forth when they understood the truth from
my lips. I know that my people have sometimes gone mad. I am
deeply sorry for [the recent killing of British soldiers in Chauri
Chaura] and I am, therefore, here to submit not to a light penalty
but to the highest penalty. I do not ask for mercy. I do not plead
any extenuating act. I am here, therefore, to invite and cheerfully
submit to the highest penalty that can be inflicted upon me for
what in law is a deliberate crime, and what appears to me to be
the highest duty of a citizen. The only course open to you, the
Judge, is either to resign your post, or inflict on me the severest
penalty if you believe that the system and law you are assisting to
administer are good for the people.

Noncooperation with evil is as much a duty as is cooperation
with good. But in the past, noncooperation has been deliberately
expressed in violence to the evildoer. I am endeavoring to show to
my compatriots that violent noncooperation only multiplies evil,
and that as evil can only be sustained by violence, withdrawal
of support of evil requires complete abstention from violence.
Nonviolence implies voluntary submission to the penalty for noncooperation with evil. I am here, therefore, to invite and submit
cheerfully to the highest penalty that can be inflicted upon me for
what in law is deliberate crime, and what appears to me to be the
highest duty of a citizen. The only course open to you, the Judge

and the assessors, is either to resign your posts and thus dissociate yourselves from evil, if you feel that the law you are called upon to administer is an evil, and that in reality I am innocent; or to inflict on me the severest penalty, if you believe that the system and the law you are assisting to administer are good for the people of this country, and that my activity, is therefore, injurious to the common weal.   —*Selected Works,* Vol. 6, 17, 19, 24

SPEECH ON THE EVE
OF THE SALT MARCH TO DANDI,
March 11, 1930

No one who believes in nonviolence as a creed need sit still. As soon as I am arrested, there should be no slackness in the enrollment of volunteers for civil disobedience. Wherever possible, civil disobedience of the salt laws should be started. These laws can be violated in three ways. It is an offense to manufacture salt wherever there are facilities for doing so. The possession and sale of contraband salt, which includes natural salt or earth salt, are also an offense. The purchasers of such salt will be equally guilty. To carry away the natural salt deposits on the seashore is likewise violation of the law. So is the hawking of such salt. In short, you may choose any one or all of these devices to break the salt monopoly.

We are, however, not to be content with this alone. There is no ban by the Congress Party and wherever the local workers have self-confidence other suitable measures may be adopted. I stress only one condition, namely, let our pledge of truth and nonviolence as the only means for the attainment of swaraj be faithfully kept. For the rest, every one has a free hand. But that does not give a license to all and sundry to carry on their own responsibility. Wherever there are local leaders, their orders should be obeyed by the people. Where there are no leaders and only a handful of people who have faith in the program, they may do what they can, if they have enough self-confidence. They have a right, nay it is their duty, to do so. The history of the world is full of instances of people who rose to leadership by sheer force of self-confidence, bravery, and tenacity. We too, if we sincerely aspire to swaraj and are impatient to attain it, should have similar self-confidence. Our ranks will swell and our hearts strengthen, as the number of our arrests by the government increases.

Much can be done in many other ways beside these. The liquor and foreign cloth shops can be picketed. We can refuse to pay taxes if we have the requisite strength. Lawyers can give up practice. The public can boycott the law courts by refraining from litigation. Government servants can resign their posts.

In the midst of the despair reigning all around, people quake with fear of losing employment. Such people are unfit for swaraj. Why this despair? The number of government servants in the country does not exceed a few hundred thousand. What about the rest? Where are they to go? Even free India will not be able to accommodate a greater number of public servants. Our starving millions can by no means afford this enormous expenditure. If therefore we are sensible enough, let us bid goodbye to government employment, no matter if it is the post of a judge or a peon. Let all who are cooperating with the government in one way or another, be it by paying taxes, keeping titles, or sending children to official schools, withdraw their cooperation in all or as many ways as possible.

You may take it as my will. It was the message that I desired to impart to you before starting on this march or for jail. I wish that there should be no suspension or abandonment of the war that commences tomorrow morning [when the 240 mile march begins] or earlier, if I am arrested before that time. I shall eagerly await the news that ten batches are ready as soon as my batch is arrested. I believe there are men and women in India to complete the work begun by me. I have faith in the righteousness of our cause and the purity of our weapons. And where the means are clean, there God is undoubtedly present with divine blessings. And where these three combine, there defeat is an impossibility. Satyagrahis, whether free or incarcerated, are ever victorious. They are vanquished only when they forsake truth and nonviolence and turn a deaf ear to the inner voice. If, therefore, there is such a thing as defeat for even satyagrahis, they alone are the cause of it. God bless you all and keep off all obstacles from the path in the struggle that begins tomorrow.

—*Selected Works,* Vol. 6, 26–28

THE JEWS IN GERMANY AND IN PALESTINE

Several letters have been received by me asking me to declare my views about the Arab-Jew question in Palestine and the persecution of the Jews in Germany. It is not without hesitation that I venture to offer my views on this very difficult question.

My sympathies are all with the Jews. I have known them intimately in South Africa. Some of them became lifelong companions. Through these friends I came to learn much of their age-long persecution. They have been the untouchables of Christianity. The parallel between their treatment by Christians and the treatment of untouchables by Hindus is very close. Religious sanction has been invoked in both cases for the justification of the inhuman treatment meted out to them. Apart from the friendships, therefore, there is the more common universal reason for my sympathy for the Jews.

But my sympathy does not blind me to the requirements of justice. The cry for the national home for the Jews does not make much appeal to me. The sanction for it is sought in the Bible and the tenacity with which the Jews have hankered after return to Palestine. Why should they not, like peoples of the earth, make that country their home where they are born and where they earn their livelihood?

Palestine belongs to the Arabs in the same sense that England belongs to the English or France to the French. It is wrong and inhuman to impose the Jews on the Arabs. What is going on in Palestine today cannot be justified by any moral code of conduct. The mandates have no sanction but that of the last war. Surely it would be a crime against humanity to reduce the proud Arabs so that Palestine can be restored to the Jews partly or wholly as their national home.

The nobler course would be to insist on a just treatment of the
Jews wherever they are born and bred. The Jews born in France
are French in precisely the same sense that Christians born in
France are French. If the Jews have no home but Palestine, will
they relish the idea of being forced to leave the other parts of the
world in which they are settled? Or do they want a double home
where they can remain at will? This cry for the national home
affords a justification for the German expulsion of the Jews.

But the German persecution of the Jews seems to have no parallel in history. The tyrants of old never went so mad as Hitler
seems to have gone. And he is doing it with religious zeal. For he
is propounding a new religion of exclusive and militant nation-
alism in the name of which any inhumanity becomes an act of
humanity to be rewarded here and hereafter. [This] crime is being visited upon his whole race with unbelievable ferocity. If there
ever could be a justifiable war in the name of and for humanity,
a war against Germany, to prevent the wanton persecution of a
whole race, would be completely justified. But I do not believe
in any war. A discussion of the pros and cons of such a war is
therefore outside my horizon or province.

But if there can be no war against Germany, even for such a
crime as is being committed against the Jews, surely there can
be no alliance with Germany. How can there be alliance between
a nation which claims to stand for justice and democracy and
one which is the declared enemy of both? Or is England drifting
toward armed dictatorship and all it means?

Germany is showing to the world how efficiently violence can
be worked when it is not hampered by any hypocrisy or weakness masquerading as humanitarianism. It is also showing how
hideous, terrible, and terrifying it looks in its nakedness.

Can the Jews resist this organized and shameless persecution?
Is there a way to preserve their self-respect and not to feel help-
less, neglected, and forlorn. I submit there is. No person who has
faith in a living God need feel helpless or forlorn. Jehovah of the
Jews is a God more personal than the God of the Christians, the
Muslims, or the Hindus, though, as a matter of fact in essence,
God is common to all and one without a second and beyond de-

scription. But as the Jews attribute personality to God and believe that God rules every action of theirs, they ought not to feel helpless. If I were a Jew and were born in Germany and earned my livelihood there, I would claim Germany as my home even as the tallest Gentile German may, and challenge him to shoot me or cast me in the dungeon. I would refuse to be expelled or to submit to discriminating treatment. And for doing this, I should not wait for the fellow Jews to join me in civil resistance but would have confidence that in the end, the rest are bound to follow my example. If one Jew or all the Jews were to accept the prescription here offered, they cannot be worse off than now. And suffering voluntarily undergone will bring them an inner strength and joy which no number of resolutions of sympathy passed in the world outside Germany can. Indeed, even if Britain, France, and America were to declare hostilities against Germany, they can bring no inner joy, no inner strength. The calculated violence of Hitler may even result in a general massacre of the Jews by way of his first answer to the declaration of such hostilities. But if the Jewish mind could be prepared for voluntary suffering, even the massacre I have imagined could be turned into a day of thanksgiving and joy that Jehovah had wrought deliverance of the race even at the hands of the tyrant. For to the God-fearing, death has no terror. It is a joyful sleep to be followed by a waking that would be all the more refreshing for the long sleep.

It is hardly necessary for me to point out that it is easier for the Jews than for the Czechs to follow my prescription. And they have in the Indian satyagraha campaign in South Africa an exact parallel. There the Indians occupied precisely the same place that the Jews occupy in Germany. The persecution had also a religious tinge. President Kruger used to say that the white Christians were the chosen of God and Indians were inferior beings created to serve whites. A fundamental clause in the Transvaal constitution was that there should be no equality between the whites and colored races including Asiatics. There too the Indians were consigned to ghettos described as locations. The other disabilities were almost of the same type as those of the Jews in Germany. The Indians, a mere handful, resorted to satyagraha without any backing from the world outside or the Indian government. Indeed the British officials tried to dissuade the satyagrahis from their contemplated step. World opinion and the Indian government came to their aid after eight years of fighting. And that too was by way of diplomatic pressure, not of a threat of war.

But the Jews of Germany can offer satyagraha under infinitely better auspices than the Indians of South Africa. The Jews are a compact, homogeneous community in Germany. They are far more gifted than the Indians of South Africa. And they have organized world opinion behind them. I am convinced that if someone with courage and vision can arise among them to lead them in nonviolent action, the winter of their despair can in the twinkling of an eye be turned into the summer of hope. And what has today become a degrading manhunt can be turned into a calm and determined stand offered by unarmed men and women possessing the strength of suffering given to them by Jehovah. It will be then a truly religious resistance offered against the godless fury of dehumanized people. The German Jews will score a lasting victory over the German Gentiles in the sense that they will have converted the latter to an appreciation of human dignity. They will have rendered service to fellow Germans and proved their title to be the real Germans as against those who are today dragging, however unknowingly, the German name into the mire.

And now a word to the Jews in Palestine. I have no doubt that they are going about it the wrong way. The Palestine of the biblical conception is not a geographical tract. It is in their hearts. But if they must look to the Palestine of geography as their national home, it is wrong to enter it under the shadow of the British gun. A religious act cannot be performed with the aid of the bayonet or the bomb. They can settle in Palestine only by the goodwill of the Arabs. They should seek to convert the Arab heart. The same God rules the Arab heart who rules the Jewish heart. They can offer satyagraha in front of the Arabs and offer themselves to be shot or thrown into the Dead Sea without raising a little finger against them. They will find the world opinion in their favor in their religious aspiration. There are hundreds of ways of reasoning with the Arabs, if they will only discard the help of the British bayonet. As it is, they are co-sharers with the British in despoiling a people who have done no wrong to them.

I am not defending the Arab excesses. I wish they had chosen the way of nonviolence in resisting what they rightly regarded as an unwarrantable encroachment upon their country. But according to the accepted canons of right and wrong, nothing can be said against the Arab resistance in the face of overwhelming odds.

Let the Jews who claim to be the chosen race prove their title by choosing the way of nonviolence for vindicating their position on earth. Every country is their home including Palestine, not by aggression but by loving service. A Jewish friend has sent me a book called *The Jewish Contribution to Civilization* by Cecil Roth. It gives a record of what the Jews have done to enrich the world's literature, art, music, drama, science, medicine, agriculture, etc. Given the will, the Jew can refuse to be treated as the outcaste of the West, to be despised or patronized. The Jew can command the attention and respect of the world by being human, the chosen creation of God, instead of fast sinking to the brute and forsaken by God. They can add to their many contributions the surpassing contribution of nonviolent action.

—Vol. 68, November 29, 1938

•

Sufferings of the nonviolent have been known to melt the stoniest hearts. I make bold to say that if the Jews can summon to their aid the soul power that comes only from nonviolence, Hitler will bow before the courage which he has never yet experienced in any large measure in his dealings with people, and which, when it is exhibited, he will accept is infinitely superior to that shown by his best storm troopers. The exhibition of such courage is only possible for those who have a living faith in the God of Truth and Nonviolence (Love).

Of course, the critics can reasonably argue that the nonviolence pictured by me is not possible for masses of humanity; it is possible only for the very few highly developed persons. I have combated that view and suggested that, given proper training and proper generalship, nonviolence can be practiced by masses of humanity.

I see, however, that my remarks are being misunderstood to mean that because I advise nonviolent resistance by the persecuted Jews, by inference I expect or would advise noninterference by the democratic powers on behalf of the Jews. I hardly need to answer this fear. Surely there is no danger of the great powers refraining from action because of anything I have said. They will, they are bound to, do all they can to free the Jews from the inhuman persecution. My appeal has force in the face of the fact that the great powers feel unable to help the Jews in an effective manner. Therefore I have offered the prescription which I know to be infallible when taken in the right manner.

The most relevant criticism, however, which I have received is this: How do I expect the Jews to accept my prescription when I know that India, where I am myself working, where I call myself the self-appointed general, has not accepted it *in toto*. My answer is: "Blessed are they that expect nothing." I belong to the category of the blessed, in this case at least. Having got the prescription and being sure of its efficacy, I felt that I would be wrong if I did not draw attention to it when I saw cases where it could be effectively applied.   —Vol. 68, December 9, 1938

•

It is highly probable that as someone writes, "A Jewish Gandhi in Germany, should one arise, could function for about five minutes and would be promptly taken to the guillotine." But that will not disprove my case or shake my belief in the efficacy of nonviolence. I can conceive the necessity of the immolation of hundreds, if not thousands, to appease the hunger of dictators who have no belief in nonviolence. Indeed, the maxim is that nonviolence is the most efficacious in front of the greatest violence. Its quality is really tested only in such cases. Sufferers need not see the result during their lifetime. They must have faith that, if their cult survives, the result is a certainty. The method of violence gives no greater guarantee than that of nonviolence. It

gives infinitely less. For the faith of the votary of nonviolence is
lacking.   —Vol. 69, May 22, 1939

A MESSAGE TO AMERICA, 1942

I am not unknown to you. I have in America perhaps the largest
number of friends in the West, not even excepting Great Britain.
British friends knowing me personally are more discerning than
the American. In America, I suffer from the well-known mal-
ady called hero worship. The good Reverend Dr. John Haynes
Holmes, until recently of the Unity Church of New York City,
without knowing me personally became my advertising agent.
Some of the nice things he said about me I never knew myself. So
I often receive embarrassing letters from America expecting me
to perform miracles. Dr. Holmes was followed much later by the
late Bishop Frederick Fisher, who knew me personally in India.
He very nearly dragged me to America but fate had ordained
otherwise, and I could not visit your vast and great country with
its wonderful people.

Moreover, you have given me a teacher in Henry David
Thoreau, who furnished me through his essay on the "Duty of
Civil Disobedience" scientific confirmation of what I was doing
in South Africa. Great Britain gave me Ruskin, whose *Unto This
Last* transformed me overnight from a lawyer and city-dweller
into a rustic living away from Durban on a farm, three miles
from the nearest railway station. Russia gave me in Tolstoy a
teacher who furnished a reasoned basis for my nonviolence. He
blessed my movement in South Africa when it was still in its in-
fancy and of whose wonderful possibilities I had yet to learn. It
was he who had prophesied in his letter to me that I was leading
a movement which was destined to bring a message of hope to
the downtrodden people of the earth.

So you will see that I have not approached the present task in
any spirit of enmity to Great Britain and the West. After having
imbibed and assimilated the message of *Unto This Last*, I could

not be guilty of approving of fascism or Nazism, whose cult is suppression of the individual and his liberty.

I invite you to read my formula of withdrawal or, as it has been popularly called, "Quit India," with this background.

I claim to be a votary of truth from my childhood. It was the most natural thing to me. A prayerful search gave me the revealing maxim "Truth is God" instead of the usual one, "God is truth." That maxim enables me to see God face to face as it were. I feel God pervade every fiber of my being. With this Truth as witness between you and me, I assert that I would not have asked my country to invite Great Britain to withdraw her rule over India, irrespective of any demand to the contrary, if I had not seen at once that for the sake of Great Britain and the Allied cause it was necessary for Britain boldly to perform the duty of freeing India from bondage. Without this essential act of tardy justice, Britain could not justify her position before the unmurmuring world conscience, which is there nevertheless. Singapore, Malaysia, and Burma taught me that the disaster must not be repeated in India. I make bold to say that it cannot be averted unless Britain trusts the people of India to use their liberty in favor of the Allied cause. By that supreme act of justice Britain would have taken away all cause for the seething discontent of India. She will turn the growing ill will into active goodwill. I submit that it is worth all the battleships and airships that your wonder-working engineers and financial resources can produce.

I know that interested propaganda has filled your ears and eyes with distorted versions of the Indian National Congress position. I have been painted as a hypocrite and enemy of Britain under disguise. My demonstrable spirit of accommodation has been described as my inconsistency, proving me to be an utterly unreliable man. If the credit I have enjoyed in America will not stand me in good stead, nothing I may argue in self-defense will carry conviction against the formidable but false propaganda that has poisoned American ears.

You have made common cause with Great Britain. You cannot therefore disown responsibility for anything that her representatives do in India. You will do a grievous wrong to the Allied cause if you do not sift the truth from the chaff while there is yet time. Just think of it. Is there anything wrong in the Congress demanding unconditional recognition of India's independence? It is being said, "But this is not the time." We say, "This is the psychological moment for that recognition." For then and then only can there be irresistible opposition to Japanese aggression. It is of immense value to the Allied cause if it is also of equal value to India. The Congress has anticipated and provided for every possible difficulty in the way of recognition. I want you to look upon the immediate recognition of India's independence as a war measure of first-class magnitude.   —Vol. 76, August 3, 1942

A MESSAGE TO AMERICA, 1946

Dislodge the false god of money called Mammon from the throne and find a corner for poor God. I think America has a very big future, but in spite of what is said to the contrary, it has a dismal future if it swears by Mammon. Mammon has never been known to be a friend of any of us to the last. He is always a false friend.
                              —*Mahatma Gandhi: Letters to Americans*,
                                                  October 21, 1946, 335

THE MISSION OF PEACE:
THE WORK OF THE UNITED NATIONS

The San Francisco Conference [at which the Charter of the United Nations would be adopted] is announced to meet shortly [on April 25, 1945]. The conference will have much to do with the world-to-be after the so-called end of the war. I very much fear that behind the structure of world security sought to be raised lurk mistrust and fear which breed war. Therefore, as a lifelong believer in peace against war, it seems well for me to record my convictions in the matter.

I reiterate my conviction that there will be no peace for the Allies or the world unless they shed their belief in the efficacy of war and its accompanying terrible deception and fraud and are determined to hammer out real peace based on freedom and equality of all races and nations. Exploitation and domination of one nation over another can have no place in a world striving to put an end to all wars. It is only in such a world that the militarily weaker nations will be free from the fear of intimidation or exploitation.

(1) An indispensable preliminary to peace is the complete freedom of India from all foreign control, not merely because it is a classic example of imperialist domination but especially because it is a big, ancient, and cultured country which has fought for its freedom since 1920 deliberately with Truth and Nonviolence as its only weapon.

(2) Freedom of India will demonstrate to all the exploited races of the earth that their freedom is very near and that in no case will they henceforth be exploited.

(3) Peace must be just. In order to be that, it must neither be punitive nor vindictive. Germany and Japan should not be humiliated. The strong are never vindictive. Therefore, fruits of peace must be equally shared. The effort then will be to turn them into friends. The Allies can prove their democracy by no other means.

(4) It follows from the foregoing that there will be no armed peace imposed upon the forcibly disarmed. All will be disarmed. There will be an international police force to enforce the lightest terms of peace. Even this retention of an international police will be a concession to human weakness, not by any means an emblem of peace.   —Vol. 79, April 17, 1945

•

Violence is bound sooner or later to exhaust itself but peace cannot issue out of such exhaustion. I am uttering God's truth when I say that unless there is a return to sanity, violent people will be swept off the face of the earth. Those who have their hands dyed deep in blood cannot build a nonviolent order for the world.

—Vol. 79, on the eve of the founding
of the United Nations, April 25, 1945

SELECTED LETTERS

Gandhi wrote tens of thousands of letters, many of which have been collected and published by the Indian government in the Collected Works. *Here are a sample of his letters.*

To Kasturbai Gandhi (from a South African prison)

I have received Mr. West's telegram today about your illness. It cuts my heart. I am very much grieved but I am not in a position to go there to nurse you. I have offered my all to the satyagraha struggle. My coming there is out of the question. I can come only if I pay the fine, which I must not.

If you keep courage and take the necessary nutrition, you will recover. If, however, my ill luck so has it that you pass away, I should only say that there would be nothing wrong in your doing so in your separation from me while I am still alive. I love you so dearly that even if you are dead, you will be alive to me. Your soul is deathless. I repeat what I have frequently told you and assure you that if you do succumb to your illness, I will not marry again. Time and again I have told you that you may quietly breathe your last with faith in God.

If you die, even that death of yours will be a sacrifice to the cause of satyagraha. My struggle is not merely political. It is religious and therefore quite pure. It does not matter much whether one dies in it or lives. I hope and expect that you will also think likewise and not be unhappy. I ask this of you.

—Vol. 9, November 9, 1908

To Manilal Gandhi (the second of Gandhi's four sons)

It is 9:30 p.m. now. It is a five day's voyage aboard ship to Cape Town. As I am tired of writing with the right hand, I write this to you with the left. As I may have to go to jail straight upon landing, I write now.

I take it that you at any rate will rejoice at my going to jail, for you have understanding. The secret of the struggle lies in going to jail cheerfully, and being happy while there.

It was good you asked the question about Phoenix [the community farm/ashram that Gandhi had set up where they were living]. First of all, we shall have to consider how we can realize the self and how serve our country. After we do this, we can explain what Phoenix is. For realizing the self, the first essential thing is to cultivate a strong moral sense. Morality means the acquisition of virtues such as fearlessness, truth, celibacy, and so on. Service is automatically rendered to the country in this process of cultivating morality. Phoenix is of great help in this process. I believe that it is very difficult to preserve morality in cities where people live in congestion and there are many temptations. That is why the wise have recommended solitary places like Phoenix. Experience is the real school. The experience you have had in Phoenix you could not have got elsewhere. Thoughts about realizing the self, again, could only occur to you there. The very fact that you have asked me such a profound question when you are a mere child shows your merit. The credit of your having been able to nurse Mr. West and others also goes to Phoenix. As most of the people in Phoenix are just beginners, you may find faults all around you. They may be there. Phoenix is not perfect, but we wish it to become so.

The Phoenix School has nothing to do with what I have said above. The school is a means to achieve our end. If it breaks down, we shall know that we are not yet fit for that kind of work. I understand your eagerness to study. My advice to you is to have patience. Concerning you, I have been thinking in various ways. I shall explain this to you when we meet. Meanwhile, have faith in Bapu ["father"]. Ask me if there is anything you have not understood.   — Vol. 10, November 24, 1909

To Esther Faering

I am here [in Motihari] for a day. I received your booklet [of St. Paul's writings on love in 1 Corinthians 13] as I was going to the station. It put me in mind of some of the happiest hours I used to have years ago in South Africa. I read the booklet years ago when I found myself in the company of some very dear Christian friends. I have read it again today with better appreciation if one may write in this manner of a sacred work like this.

For me, truth and love are interchangeable terms. You may not know that the Gujarati for passive resistance is truth-force. I have variously defined it as truth-force, love-force, or soul-force. But truly there is nothing in words.

What one has to do is to live a life of love in the midst of the hate we see everywhere. And we cannot do it without unconquerable faith in its efficacy.

A great queen named Mirabai lived two or three hundred years ago. She forsook her husband and everything and lived a life of absolute love. Her husband at last became her devotee. We often sing in the ashram some fine hymns composed by her. You shall hear and one of these days sing them when you come to the ashram.

Thank you for the precious gift. I need such thoughts as are contained in the work.   — Vol. 13, June 11, 1917

To Hermann Kallenbach

I have been irregular of late. I have been wandering so much that I never have the leisure to write love letters especially when they get lost. From you I have had only three letters during the past three months. Polak has however written to me about you and so has Miss Winterbottom. How often do I now want to hug you. Daily do I have novel experiences here which I should like you to share with me.

But this monstrous war never seems to be ending. All the peace talk only enhances the agony. However, like all human institutions it must have an end, and our friendship must be a poor affair if it cannot bide its time and be all the stronger and purer for the weary waiting.

And what is this physical form after all? As I was whizzing through the air [on the train] yesterday and looking at the trees, I saw that beneath all the change that these mighty trees daily underwent, there was a something that persisted. Every leaf has its own separate life. It drops and withers. But the tree lives on. Every tree falls in process of time or under the cruel axe, but the forest of which the tree is but a part lives. And so with us, leaves of the human tree. We may wither, but the eternal in us lives on, changeless and endless. I derived much comfort last evening as I was thus musing. The thoughts went on to you and I sighed, but I regained self-possession and said to myself, "I know my friend not for his form but for that which informs him."

—Vol. 14, December 21, 1917

To Jamnalal Bajaj

As I proceed in my search for Truth, it grows upon me that Truth comprehends everything. It is not in nonviolence, but nonviolence is in Truth. What is perceived by a pure heart and intellect is Truth for that moment. Cling to it, and it enables one to reach pure Truth. There is no question there of divided duty. But often enough it is difficult to decide what is nonviolence. For instance, the use of disinfectants is violence, and yet we cannot do without it. We have to live a life of nonviolence in the midst of a world of violence, and that is possible only if we cling to Truth. That is how I deduce nonviolence from Truth. Out of Truth emanate love, tenderness, humility. Votaries of Truth have to be humble as the dust. Their humility increases with their observance of Truth. I see this every moment of my life. I have a much more vivid sense of Truth and of my own littleness than I had a year ago. The wonderful implication of the great Truth, "Brahma is real; all else unreal," grows on me from day to day. It teaches us patience. This will purge us of harshness and add to our tolerance. It will make us magnify the mole-hills of our errors into mountains and minimize the mountains of others' errors into mole-hills. The body persists because of egoism. The utter extinction of the body of egoism is moksha [salvation]. The one who has achieved this will be the very image of Truth, or one may call it Brahman. Therefore, the loving name of God is Dasanudasa, "Servant of Servants."

Wife, children, friends, possessions — all should be held sub-servient to Truth. Each one of these should be sacrificed in the search for Truth. Only then can one be a satyagrahi. I have thrown myself into this movement with a view to making the observance of this principle comparatively easy, and it is with the same object that I do not hesitate to plunge people like you in it. Its outward form is Hind swaraj. This swaraj is being delayed because there is yet to be found a satyagrahi of that type. This, however, need not dismay us. It should spur us on to greater effort.

You have made yourself my fifth son. But I am striving to be worthy. May God help me, and may I be worthy of it in this very life.   — From Sabarmati Central Prison, *Selected Works,* Vol. 5, March 16, 1922, 144–45

To Amiya Chakravarti

How can I help you find peace? It can only come from within and by waiting upon God and trusting God with implicit faith. No one need ever feel lonely who feels the living presence of God near him and in him. Whatever peace I have found has been found by increasing faith in the hand of God being in every-thing. Calamities then cease to be calamities. They test our faith and steadfastness. May you also find your peace in the midst of seeming strife.   —Vol. 30, June 11, 1926

To Mirabehn

I have your letter about prayer. The letter is beautiful.

Love means infinite patience, and exactly in the measure that we become impatient of our own weaknesses, we have to be patient with regard to the weaknesses of our neighbors. We easily enough see their weaknesses, but we have absolutely no knowledge of their striving to overcome them.

That the prayer meetings at the ashram are not what they should be — full of fragrance and reality — is really due to my own shortcomings of which neither you nor anybody else can have any notion whatsoever. The value of prayer dawned upon me very late in life, and as I have a fair capacity for imposing discipline upon myself, I have by patient and painful striving been able now for some years to conform to the outward form.

But do I conform to the spirit? My answer is: No. While it is true that life would be insipid for me without prayer, I am not absorbed in the message of prayer at prayer times. The mind wanders where it would in spite of incessant striving. If I could but lose myself in prayer like the great Ali, you will not have to make the complaint that you have rightly registered in your letter.

You will not now wonder why I am patient with those who are slack even in attending to the external form. I therefore tremble to impose any iron rule upon the people. Knowing my own weakness, I sympathize with theirs, and hope that if I grow, they must grow with me. You will now understand more than ever what I have so often said to so many people: I must be measured, not by what I appear personally, but by how I appear in the lives of the people at the ashram. The ashram, especially when I am withdrawn from it, is really the only infallible guide to a knowledge of me.   —Vol. 34, July 20, 1927

To Dietrich Bonhoeffer

I have your letter. If you and your friend have enough money for return passage and can pay your expenses here, say, at the rate of 100 rupees each month, you can come whenever you like. The sooner the better so as to get the benefit of such cold weather as we get here. The 100 rupees per month I have calculated is the outside limit for those who can live simply. It may cost you even half the amount. It all depends upon how the climate here agrees with you.

With reference to your desire to share my daily life, I may say that you will be staying with me if I am out of prison and settled in one place when you come. But otherwise, if I am traveling or if I am in prison, you will have to be satisfied with remaining in or near one of the institutions that are being conducted under my supervision. If you can stay in any of the institutions I have in mind and if you can live on the simple vegetarian food that these institutions can supply you, you will have nothing to pay for your boarding and lodging.

—Vol. 59, November 1, 1934

To Daniel Oliver

I have no message to give except this: that there is no deliverance for any people on this earth or for all the people of this earth except through truth and nonviolence in every walk of life without any exceptions. And this is based on an unbroken experience extending practically over half a century.

—Vol. 65, June 11, 1937

To Adolf Hitler

Friends have been urging me to write to you for the sake of humanity. But I have resisted their request, because of the feeling that any letter from me would be an impertinence. Something tells me that I must not calculate and that I must make my appeal for whatever it may be worth.

It is quite clear that you are today the one person in the world who can prevent a war which may reduce humanity to the savage state. Must you pay that price for an object however worthy it may appear to you to be? Will you listen to the appeal of one who has deliberately shunned the method of war not without considerable success? Any way, I anticipate your forgiveness, if I have erred in writing to you.   —Vol. 70, July 23, 1939

•

I own no foes. My business in life has been for the past thirty-three years to enlist the friendship of the whole of humanity by befriending humanity, irrespective of race, color, or creed.

I hope you will have the time and desire to know how a good portion of humanity who have been living under the influence of that doctrine of universal friendship view your action. Your own writings and pronouncements and those of your friends and admirers leave no room for doubt that many of your acts are monstrous and unbecoming of human dignity, especially in the estimation of people like me who believe in universal friendliness. Such are your humiliation of Czechoslovakia, the rape of Poland, and the swallowing of Denmark. I am aware that your view of life regards such spoliations as virtuous acts. But we have been taught from childhood to regard them as acts degrading humanity. Hence we cannot possibly wish success to your arms.

But ours is a unique position. We resist British imperialism no less than Nazism. If there is a difference, it is in degree. One-fifth of the human race has been brought under the British heel by means that will not bear scrutiny. Our resistance to it does not mean harm to the British people. We seek to convert them, not to defeat them on the battlefield. Ours is an unarmed revolt against the British rule. But whether we convert them or not, we are determined to make their rule impossible by nonviolent non-cooperation. It is a method in its nature indefensible. It is based on the knowledge that no spoiler can compass his end without a certain degree of cooperation, willing or compulsory, of the victim. Our rulers may have our land and bodies but not our souls. They can have the former only by complete destruction of every Indian — man, woman, and child. That all may not rise to that degree of heroism and that a fair amount of frightfulness can bend the back of revolt is true, but the argument would be beside the point. For, if a fair number of men and women be found in India who would be prepared without any ill will against the spoilers to lay down their lives rather than bend the knee to them, they would have shown the way to freedom from the tyranny of violence. I ask you to believe me when I say that you will find an unexpected number of such men and women in India. They have been having that training for the past twenty years.

We have been trying for the past half a century to throw off British rule. The movement of independence has been never so strong as now. The most powerful political organization, the Indian National Congress, is trying to achieve this end. We have attained a very fair measure of success through nonviolent effort.

We were groping for the right means to combat the most organized violence in the world, which the British power represents. You have challenged it. It remains to be seen which is the better organized, the German or the British. We know what the British heel means for us and the non-European races of the world. But we would never wish to end the British rule with German aid. We have found in nonviolence a force which, if organized, can without a doubt match itself against a combination of all the most violent forces in the world. In nonviolent technique, as I have said, there is no such thing as defeat. It is all "Do or Die" without killing or hurting. It can be used practically without money and obviously without the aid of the science of destruction which you have brought to such perfection.

It is a marvel to me that you do not see that it is nobody's monopoly. If not the British, some other power will certainly improve upon your method and beat you with your own weapon. You are leaving no legacy to your people of which they would feel proud. They cannot take pride in a recital of cruel deeds, however skillfully planned.

I therefore appeal to you in the name of humanity to stop the war. You will lose nothing by referring all the matters of dispute between you and Britain to an international tribunal of your joint choice. If you attain success in the war, it will not prove that you were in the right. It will only prove that your power of destruction was greater. Whereas an award by an impartial tribunal will show as far as it is humanly possible which party was in the right.

You know that not long ago I made an appeal to every Briton to accept my method of nonviolent resistance. I did it because the British know me as a friend though a rebel. I am a stranger to you and your people. I have not the courage to make you the appeal I made to every Briton. Not that it would not apply to you with the same force as to the British.

During this season when the hearts of the peoples of Europe yearn for peace, we have suspended even our own peaceful struggle. Is it too much to ask you to make an effort for peace during a time which may mean nothing to you personally but which must mean much to the millions of Europeans whose

dumb cry for peace I hear, for my ears are attuned to hearing
the dumb millions?   —Vol. 73, December 24, 1940
                    The British government would not allow this letter
                    to be delivered or made public.

To Franklin D. Roosevelt

I just missed coming to your great country. I have the privilege
of having numerous friends there both known and unknown to
me. Many of my compatriots have received and are still receiving
higher education in America. I know too that several have taken
shelter there. I have profited greatly by the writings of Thoreau
and Emerson. I say this to tell you how much I am connected
with your country.

Of Great Britain, I need say nothing beyond mentioning that
in spite of my intense dislike of British rule, I have numerous
personal friends in England whom I love as dearly as my own
people. I had my legal education there. I have therefore nothing
but good wishes for your country and Great Britain.

You will therefore accept my word that my present proposal,
that the British should unreservedly and without reference to the
wishes of the people of India immediately withdraw their rule, is
prompted by the friendliest intention. I would like to turn into
goodwill the ill will which, whatever may be said to the contrary,
exists in India toward Great Britain.

My personal position is clear. I hate all war. If therefore I could
persuade my compatriots, they would make a most effective and
decisive contribution in favor of an honorable peace. But I know
that all of us have not a living faith in nonviolence.

The policy of the Indian National Congress, largely guided
by me, has been one of nonembarrassment to Britain, consistently with the honorable working of the Congress, admittedly
the largest political organization with the longest standing in
India. The British policy has driven me to the proposal I have
made. I hold that the full acceptance of my proposal and that
alone can put the Allied cause on an unassailable basis. I venture
to think that the Allied declaration that the Allies are fighting to

make the world safe for freedom of the individual and for democracy sounds hollow so long as India and, for that matter, Africa are exploited by Great Britain, and America has the Negro problem in her own home. But in order to avoid all complications, in my proposal I have confined myself only to India. If India becomes free, the rest must follow.

So far as India is concerned, we must become free even as America and Great Britain are. —Vol. 76, July 1, 1942

To Jawaharlal Nehru

I have been desirous of writing to you for many days but have not been able to do so before today. The first thing I want to write about is the difference of outlook between us. If the difference is fundamental then I feel the public should also be made aware of it. It would be detrimental to our work for independence to keep them in the dark.

I am convinced that if India is to attain true freedom and through India the world also, then sooner or later the fact must be recognized that people will have to live in villages, not in cities; in huts, not in palaces. Millions of people will never be able to live at peace with each other in towns, cities, and palaces. They will have no recourse but to resort to both violence and untruth. I hold that without truth and nonviolence there can be nothing but destruction for humanity. We can realize truth and nonviolence only in the simplicity of village life.

I must not fear if the world today is going the wrong way. It may be that India too will go that way and like the proverbial moth burn itself eventually in the flame around which it dances more and more furiously. But it is my bound duty up to my last breath to try to protect India and through India the entire world from such a doom. The essence of what I have said is that humanity should rest content with what are its real needs and become self-sufficient. If humanity does not have this control, it cannot save itself. After all, the world is made up of individuals just as it is the drops of water that constitute the ocean. I have said nothing new. This is a well-known truth.

While I admire modern science, I find that it is the old looked at in the true light of modern science which should be reclothed and refashioned aright. You must not imagine that I am envisaging our village life as it is today. The village of my dreams is still in my mind. After all, we all live in the world of our dreams. My ideal village will contain intelligent human beings. They will not live in dirt and darkness as animals. Men and women will be free and able to hold their own against any one in the world. There will be neither plague, nor cholera, nor smallpox. No one will be idle. No one will wallow in luxury. Everyone will have to contribute a quota of manual labor. I do not want to draw a large-scale picture in detail. It is possible to envisage railways, post and telegraph offices, etc. For me it is material to obtain the real article and the rest will fit into the picture.

I want our position vis-à-vis each other to be clearly understood by us for two reasons. First, the bond that unites us is not only political work. It is immeasurably deeper and quite unbreakable. Therefore it is that I earnestly desire that in the political field also we should understand each other clearly. Second, neither of us thinks himself useless. We both live for the cause of India's freedom, and we would both gladly die for it. We are not in need of the world's praise. Whether we get praise or blame is immaterial to us. There is no room for praise in service. I want to live to 125 for the service of India but I must admit that I am now an old man. You are much younger in comparison, and I have therefore named you as my heir. I must, however, understand my heir and my heir should understand me. Then alone shall I be content.

—Vol. 81, October 5, 1945

8

Epilogue

IF ONE GAINS SPIRITUALLY,
THE WHOLE WORLD GAINS

I do not believe that we may gain spiritually and those that surround us suffer. I believe in the essential unity of humanity and for that matter of all that lives. Therefore, I believe that if one person gains spiritually, the whole world gains with that person, and if one person falls, the whole world falls to that extent.

— *All Men Are Brothers,* 107

PEACE COMES ONLY
THROUGH SATYAGRAHA

Deep inside me I have an ever growing faith that in the midst of this universal destruction due to bloodshed, I am carrying on an absolutely innocuous struggle which, however, is pregnant with great potentialities.

In a satyagraha movement, the saying that God is the giver of the result is literally true. Therefore, it is faith that sustains me, and it is faith that must sustain the other satyagrahis. We have only begun the battle. The real test, the real suffering, has yet to come. Let me repeat for the thousandth time that, in this long and arduous struggle, quality alone will count, never quantity. In this there is no room for hatred.

I venture to say that only through this satyagraha struggle can we hope for permanent world peace. Peace can never come through war.   — Vol. 73, March 29, 1941

NO MORE WAR, NO MORE GREED

An armed conflict between nations horrifies us. But the economic war is no better than an armed conflict. This is like a surgical operation. An economic war is prolonged torture. And its ravages are no less terrible than those depicted in the literature on war properly so called. We think nothing of the other because we are used to its deadly effects.

Many of us in India shudder to see blood spilled. Many of us resent cow-slaughter, but we think nothing of the slow torture through which by our greed we put our people and cattle. But because we are used to this lingering death, we think no more about it.

The movement against war is sound. I pray for its success. But I cannot help the gnawing fear that the movement will fail, if it does not touch the root of all evil — greed.

Will America, England, and the other great nations of the West continue to exploit the so-called weaker or uncivilized races and hope to attain peace that the whole world is pining for? Or will Americans continue to prey upon one another, have commercial rivalries, and yet expect to dictate peace to the world?

Not till the spirit is changed can the form be altered. The form is merely an expression of the spirit within. We may succeed in seemingly altering the form, but the alteration will be a mere make-believe if the spirit within remains unalterable. A whitened sepulcher still conceals beneath it the rotting flesh and bone.

Far be it from me to discount or underrate the great effort that is being made in the West to kill the war spirit. Mine is merely a word of caution as from a fellow-seeker who has been striving in his own humble manner after the same thing, maybe in a different way, no doubt on a much smaller scale. But if the experiment demonstrably succeeds on the smaller field and, if those who are working on the larger field have not overtaken me, it will at least pave the way for a similar experiment on a large field.

I observe in the limited field in which I find myself that unless I can reach the hearts of men and women, I am able to do nothing. I observe further that so long as the spirit of hate persists in some shape or other, it is impossible to establish peace or to gain our freedom by peaceful effort. We cannot love one another if we hate the English. We cannot love the Japanese and hate the English. We must either let the Law of Love rule us through and through or not at all.

Love among ourselves based on hatred of others breaks down under the slightest pressure. The fact is such love is never real love. It is an armed peace. And so it will be in this great movement in the West against war. War will only be stopped when the conscience of humanity has become sufficiently elevated to recognize the undisputed supremacy of the Law of Love in all the walks of life. Some say this will never come to pass. I shall retain the faith till the end of my earthly existence that it shall come to pass.   —Vol. 31, November 8, 1926

TAKE UP NONVIOLENCE
OR WE ARE DOOMED

It is open to the great powers to take up nonviolence any day and cover themselves with glory and earn the eternal gratitude of posterity. If they or any of them can shed the fear of destruction, if they disarm themselves, they will automatically help the rest to regain their sanity. But then these great powers have to give up imperialistic ambitions and exploitation of the so-called uncivilized nations of the earth and revise their mode of life. It means a complete revolution. Great nations can hardly be expected in the ordinary course to move spontaneously in a direction the reverse of the one they have followed and according to their notion of value, from victory to victory. But miracles have happened before and may happen even in this very prosaic age. Who can dare limit God's power of undoing wrong?

One thing is certain. If the mad race for armaments continues, it is bound to result in a slaughter such as has never occurred in history. If there is a victor left the very victory will be a living death for the nation that emerges victorious. There is no escape from the impending doom save through a bold and unconditional acceptance of the nonviolent method with all its glorious implications.   —Vol. 68, November 5 and 12, 1938

PEACE COMES THROUGH A LIVING FAITH

Not to believe in the possibility of permanent peace is to disbelieve the Godliness of human nature. Methods hitherto adopted have failed because rock-bottom sincerity on the part of those who have striven has been lacking. Not that they have realized this lack. Peace is unattainable by a partial performance of conditions, even as chemical combination is impossible without complete fulfillment of the conditions of attainment. If recognized leaders of humanity who have control over the engines of destruction were wholly to renounce their use with full knowledge of the implications, permanent peace could be obtained. This is clearly impossible without the great powers of the earth renouncing their imperialistic designs. This again seems impossible without these great nations ceasing to believe in soul-destroying competition and to desire to multiply wants and therefore increase their material possessions.

It is my conviction that the root of evil is want of a living faith in a living God. It is a first-class human tragedy that peoples of the earth who claim to believe in the message of Jesus whom they describe as the Prince of Peace show little of that belief in actual practice. It is painful to see sincere Christians limiting the scope of Jesus' message to individuals. I have been taught from my childhood, and I have tested the truth by experience, that the primary virtues of humanity can be cultivated by the meanest of the human species. It is this undoubted universal possibility that distinguishes the human from the rest of God's creation. If even one great nation were unconditionally to perform the supreme act of renunciation, many of us would see in our lifetime visible peace established on earth.

— Vol. 62, May 16, 1936; see also, June 16, 1938

PEACE COMES FROM THE HEART

I request that you join me in the prayer that peace and love may again be established in India and the world and all may become brothers and sisters. Today there is no peace to be seen anywhere in the world. Peace cannot be established with the help of money. So long as there is no peace in the heart, there can be no peace outside. Only when peace issues from within the heart and is expressed through the eyes, words, and actions of people can we say that peace has been established. A person of peace can live happily even in a mud hut and has no thought of the morrow, for it is only God who knows what will happen on the morrow.

— Speech at a prayer meeting at a refugee camp,
a few weeks before his assassination,
Vol. 90, January 3, 1948

THE WORLD OF TOMORROW, A WORLD OF NONVIOLENCE

Perhaps never before has there been so much speculation about the future as there is today. Will our world always be a world of violence? Will there always be poverty, starvation, and misery? Will we have a firmer and wider belief in religion, or will the world be godless? If there is to be a great change in society, how will that change be wrought? By war or revolution? Or will it come peacefully?

Different people give different answers to these questions, each of us drawing the plan of tomorrow's world as we hope and wish it to be. I answer not only out of belief but out of conviction. The world of tomorrow will be, must be, a society based on nonviolence. That is the first law. Out of it, all other blessings will flow. It may seem a distant goal, an impractical Utopia. But it is not in the least unobtainable, since it can be worked for here and now. An individual can adopt the way of life of the future — the nonviolent way — without having to wait for others to do so. And if an individual can do it, cannot whole groups of individuals? Whole nations? People often hesitate to make a beginning, because they feel that the objective cannot be achieved in its entirety. This attitude of mind is precisely our greatest obstacle to progress — an obstacle that each of us, if we only will it, can clear away.

Equal distribution — the second great law of tomorrow's world as I see it — grows out of nonviolence. It implies not that the world's goods shall be arbitrarily divided up, but that each person shall have the wherewithal to supply their natural needs, no more.

Does not this whole idea of nonviolence imply a change in human nature? And does history at any time record such a change? Emphatically it does. Many an individual has turned from the mean, personal, acquisitive point of view to one that sees society as a whole and works for its benefit. If there has been such a change in one person, there can be the same change in many.

I see no poverty in the world of tomorrow, no wars, no revolutions, no bloodshed. And in that world, there will be a faith in God greater and deeper than ever in the past. The very existence of the world in a broad sense depends on religion. All attempts to root it out will fail.   —*Selected Works*, Vol. 6, 260–62

THE GANDHI TALISMAN

I will give you a talisman. Whenever you are in doubt, or when the self becomes too much with you, apply the following test.

Recall the face of the poorest and the weakest person whom you have seen, and ask yourself if the next step you contemplate is going to be of any use to that person. Will that person gain anything by it? Will it restore that person to a control over his or her own life and destiny? In other words, will it lead to freedom for the hungry and spiritually starving millions?

Then you will find your doubts and your self melting away.

—Vol. 89, August 1947